ARTHURIAN LITERATURE

I

Arthurian Literature
I

Edited by Richard Barber

D. S. BREWER · ROWMAN & LITTLEFIELD

Published by D. S. Brewer
an imprint of Boydell & Brewer Ltd
PO Box 9, Woodbridge, Suffolk IP12 3DF
and Rowman and Littlefield
81 Adams Drive, Totowa, N.J.07512

ISBN 0 85991 081 4

US ISBN 0 8476 7051 1

Printed in Great Britain by St Edmundsbury Press
Bury St Edmunds, Suffolk

CONTENTS

PREFACE

In view of the increasing interest in the Arthurian legends, it is perhaps surprising that no periodical exists devoted exclusively to studies in this field, except for the International Arthurian Society's own Bibliographical Bulletin. The present publication is designed to remedy this, but only in part: *Arthurian Literature* will be primarily devoted to essays of what might be termed monograph length, of 20,000 words and upwards, though this will not be a hard and fast rule. Its scope, as the essay by Karl Heinz Göller in this volume indicates, will not be restricted to purely medieval studies, but will cover all aspects of Arthurian literature, including its influence on art and music.

In view of the disparity of topics covered, it is not practical to index each volume; instead, a cumulative index will appear at the end of every fifth volume. There will be no reviews of books, though this does not exclude the possibility of survey articles on current work in particular fields. Offers of contributions should be addressed to the editor, care of Boydell and Brewer Ltd, PO Box 9, Woodbridge, Suffolk IP12 3DF.

Professor Toshiyuki Takamiya of Keio University and Dr Tony Hunt of St Andrews University have kindly agreed to act as advisory editors for future volumes; it is only fair to point out that the choice of contents of the present volume is the sole responsibility of the editor.

RICHARD BARBER
September 1981

I

CHRETIEN DE TROYES AND ENGLAND*

Constance Bullock-Davies

I

... inutile de supposer, comme en l'a fait, qu'il a voyagé en Angleterre ou en Armorique. Jean Frappier, *Chrétien de Troyes, l'homme et l'oeuvre.*[1]

Il a, sans doute, voyagé en Angleterre et peut-être séjourné à Nantes. Alexandre Micha, *Dictionnaire des Lettres Françaises.*[2]

In the world of speculative research, diametrically opposed views such as these are by no means rare. Whether Chrétien de Troyes visited this country has been a moot point for quite a long while but, as far as I know, no one has seriously examined in detail the clues in his poems which suggest that he did. I have set myself this task, and in the prosecution of it have discovered a number of unexpected facts which go far to substantiate M. Micha's claim.

I have made every effort to approach the problem with no preconceived idea of Chrétien's status or of his activities, since there is no indisputable evidence of either the one or the other. Nor have I allowed probability to figure too largely

* I am most grateful to Mr R. W. Barber, who read this piece of work in manuscript. Thanks to his helpful comments and suggestions I have been able to clarify my argument in several ways.

I am also deeply indebted to Miss Frances Lynch of the Department of History (Archaeology), Bangor, who prepared and drew the plan of Windsor Castle for me.

1. Paris 1957, 57.

2. Paris 1964, 182.

in my arguments, because I think it presumptuous to attempt to describe the life of a man of whom nothing is known for certain and who lived so long ago. For us Chrétien lives only in his writings and even these cannot be wholly reliable: there is no original manuscript of any of his poems, the majority of those extant being of the thirteenth century. M. Micha's summing up of the state of them constitutes a salutary, even sardonic, warning to all who study Chrétien's work:

> Le scribe qui recopiait un texte biblique ne s'écartait pas de ce qu'il avait sous les yeux: c'eut été péché que d'en changer un iota. L'ouvrier de librairie profane, lui, n'a point ces scruples: il retouche le texte, il arrange, il coupe, il allonge . . . Mais enfin ces éditions existent, et même quand le scribe n'a pas eu une idee arretée, ces réfections de chaque instant sont là pour nous prouver avec quelle désinvolture et quel irrespect les ateliers traitaient l'oeuvre du maitre, avec quelle facilité et complaisance les lecteurs acceptaient ces retapages de textes, ces travestis de la pensée de l'auteur. Ni les uns ni les autres n'avaient mêmes exigences que nous; il semble que l'oeuvre, une fois signée du nom de l'auteur et lui assurant la gloire de la première invention, tombe dans le domaine public et devienne impunément la proie de ces mille rimailleurs qui exercent le métier de copiste. L'un a fourni le thème, les autres vont, là-dessus, faire fleurir les innombrables variations de détail, pauvres fleurs en vérité, malgre la dexterité de certains d'entre eux.

'What are we to do,' he concludes, 'when we present a new edition of a text to the modern reader? Shall it be one by a thirteenth century scribe or one by a philologist of the twentieth. . . où est la différence?'[3]

Bearing in mind these difficulties, I have concentrated on elucidating the statements in the texts as we now have them and have paid particular attention to variant readings. How delicate the operation has been may be readily understood if parallel circumstances in our own day were to be postulated. So much is taken for granted and therefore left unsaid in any

3. *La tradition manuscrite des romans de Chrétien de Troyes*, Geneva 1966, 387, 389.

tale of contemporary life, that readers of it in a different century are liable to miss half the nuances and, out of an ardent desire to understand, are apt to ascribe undue importance and sometimes far-fetched meaning to the simplest, most commonplace statements. I have tried to interpret what Chrétien has said about this country in the light of as much strictly relevant, authentic knowledge of his period as is available. It is necessarily fitful and incomplete. Between nim and me lie eight centuries with their lost manuscripts, inexpert copyists, meddlers with original texts and, above all, long, memory-engulfing years. Like a knight about to enter the lists, I fervently echo his prayer: *Or le bon Diex me soit en aidance.*

II

Arthurian romance, as it has come down to us in Old French and Middle English literature, is an anachronism. A writer in any period either chooses his subject deliberately from source-material to hand or is driven by inner compulsion to create a tale out of his own knowledge, experience and imagination. Both methods of composition are subject to influences exerted by the author's social and cultural environment. They are also, although to a lesser extent, subject to contemporary demand, for it is the followers or imitators of a popular mode of writing who keep the general appetite fed; an original author usually departs from accepted fashions and ends by shaping succeeding taste.

Every story is bound to its own time-scheme within its own historical context, whether that context be factual or fictitious. Nowadays this is a self-evident truth, because we possess both a knowledge of the past and an awareness of anachronism which prevent us from unconsciously delineating the past totally in terms of the present. Historical narrative, as we know it, did not exist in the twelfth century; all ancient tales were re-told in a contemporary setting. What is peculiar about the Arthurian tales of Chrétien de Troyes is that the contemporary setting came to be more than a naive substitute for the past. Both Chrétien and his audience appear to have been constantly aware of the fact that Celtic

3

stories belonged to a remote past, yet exactly *what* past it was they were not at all sure, and evidently did not care, for Arthur was invested with the panoply of feudal military society as it was in the twelfth century; and there he has remained. At the same time, it was recognised that he was not of it; he belonged to an unreal period of human history. Despite the benefits of present-day archaeological research and unremitting scholarly speculation, the world of Arthur, the 'king' as distinct from that of Arthur, the post-Roman *dux bellorum*, remains unidentifiable; and no wonder, for it never existed. Chrétien and his contemporaries, including Geoffrey of Monmouth, transformed the nebulous, Celtic warrior-leader into an idealised monarch, a picture of royal perfectibility as conceived by the twelfth-century mind.

It has been said that Chrétien was the originator of Arthurian 'romance'. It may well be so. No one knows what his immediate sources were. Unfortunately, Geoffrey of Monmouth had already plotted the general geography of Arthurian Britain to which Chrétien in some of his tales dutifully pays heed; but there were sources of Arthurian story other than Geoffrey's *Historia Regum Britanniae* which he may or may not have known. In the terms used by Ailred of Rievaulx they include dramatic performances (*tragoediae*), songs (*carmina*) and narratives (*fabulae*)[4] recited with appropriate histrionic voice-change and gesture. The definitions implicit in these terms are important, because they testify to a range of art-forms which have been only vaguely reflected in what literature has been preserved but they must have been common among the minstrels who performed them. Geoffrey's arbitrary, tailored version of ancient British history has obscured, probably for ever, the wider tracts of Arthur's realm as well as a fuller embodiment of his personality. When dealing with the vexed problem of sources it is desirable to keep this fact in mind. As any writer with a keen eye to his profession and reputation, Chrétien could have picked up his raw material wherever he found it, whether it was in Latin or in French, in an old book in a cathedral aumbry or by word of mouth from a boon companion. When he received a commission, as in the cases of *Le Chévalier de la Charrete* and *Le Conte du Graal*, his materials were provided

4. *Speculum Charitatis*, PL cxcv, 562.

4

for him, although it is not known in what form or language these were. What is obvious – and astonishing – is that there is nothing to show that he knew anything at all about genuine Celtic story and background except what was in his immediate source or what he may have absorbed from the literature and minstrelsy of the Britons/Bretons around him. He came to the *matière de Bretagne* with a foreigner's outlook and found it refreshingly new and full of possibilities. To have re-told the stories precisely as he had heard or read them would have made him a mouthpiece for something he really did not understand and which, because it was second-hand, would have been lacking in the original gleam of vitality. Instead, he refashioned them to suit both his own imaginative needs and the taste of his prospective audiences; which means that he transferred alien concepts into French thought. Things Celtic offered him a new pattern of thinking. He abstracted as much of the essence as he understood and presented it in the only way he could, namely, in terms of his twelfth-century Frenchness. In this sense, medieval Arthurian romance, as it stemmed from Chrétien, was a hybrid from the start. It was and it was not British/Welsh; it was and it was not ancient. This paradox becomes startlingly apparent and intelligible when attention is focussed upon his use of place-names.

The Welsh place-names in his work are, with one or two rather suspect exceptions, all to be found in Geoffrey's *Historia* and were platitudinously common to all known versions of Arthurian stories post-Geoffrey. As far as the topography of *Celtic* Britain is concerned, Chrétien could have composed his romances without ever having visited this country. He either accepted the names from the source he was using or else invested his tale with a cloak of recognisable Galfredian or other 'British' authenticity. With regard to *English* place-names, however, the situation is quite different. These he uses not only with the confidence of one who has personal knowledge of them but in a manner that betrays a good deal of his method of creative composition. *Cligès* provides an excellent example.

If the reader concentrates on the details of the narrative as it unfolds, he soon begins to realise that he is being given descriptions of voyages and journeyings of foreigners, or, more precisely, of Frenchmen, to and from the south of England. Their every movement can be paralleled in the

5

movements of the English court or business trips of merchants. Since the story is supposed to belong to the miasmic time of King Arthur, the adventures of Alexander and later of Cligès abound in the special brand of anachronisms which Chrétien's Arthurian romances inevitably produced. Had the tales been ones of purely civil rather than of military life, his task would have been infinitely more difficult; but, up to the time of the adoption of gunpowder in war by western nations, the conduct of fighting remained basically unchanged; military engines and tactics common in Roman times were used throughout the Middle Ages, so that the transference of ideas about military life from one era to another was comparatively easy. Arthur, like Achilles, Hector, Alexander the Great or Caesar, was a fabulously renowned warrior. He presided, in the same way as Henry II or any other medieval monarch did, over a war-orientated society. It was of no great importance, at any rate in fiction, that fashions in arms and armour should have changed somewhat with the passage of time. Military virtues, as well as military tactics, were constant. Consequently, it was not difficult to conceive of Arthur as existing simultaneously in the past and the present, as fighting against Roman tribunes and emperors and presiding over tournaments. When Alexander and Cligès, supposedly living in Arthur's time, came, each in turn, to visit the great Celtic king, it seemed quite natural that they should land at Southampton and make straight for Winchester where the then most powerful king in Europe, Henry II, held court.

The details relevant to England in *Cligès* are such that they could hardly have been extracted from books or picked up by mere hearsay in France. In the first place, the oddity of the plot needs to be considered. Whatever motivated Chrétien's composition of the first part of the story, it faced him with the problem of tacking it on to the tale he had found in a volume in Beauvais cathedral library. This was a Graeco-Byzantine tale which, for some reason or other, he decided to turn into an Arthurian romance, presumably because, in composing tales about Arthur, he was, in modern journalistic parlance, 'onto a good thing'. The problem was, how to persuade his audience/readers that this old Eastern European story was not what it seemed to be, but an up-to-the-minute piece of Arthurian entertainment. The way in which he solved it was characteristically ingenious: he conceived the bright idea of making the hero, Cligès, Sir Gawain's nephew, thus binding him in blood relationship to Arthur himself, who was Gawain's uncle. A bald statement to this effect at the commencement of a Graeco-Byzantine tale would have been callow in the extreme, to say nothing of its being incredible by even medieval standards. The Graeco-Byzantine tale needed some preliminary Arthurian atmosphere and trappings to render it plausibly Celtic. Therefore, how Cligès came to be half-Greek, half-Briton, had to be convincingly explained; hence the account of Alexander's exploits in what Chrétien was pleased to call at first, 'Britain and Cornwall', perhaps a faint echo of Geoffrey's Britain or the area of the young Tristan's activity, for Cornwall does not figure in *Cligès*. In reality, the first part of *Cligès* seems to have been based on Chrétien's personal experience of southern England and his imaginative genius with regard to Arthurian fiction.

It is possible to trace the thread of personal experience, and I include personal observation as well, from the very beginning of the story. The first happy blunder is that Alexander, in order to win renown, 'went from Greece to England' *'ala de Grece en Engleterre'* (16); but, like Wace and so many other writers of the time, Chrétien immediately puts matters right by saying that England used to be called Britain 'then' *'lors'* (17). Apparently Chrétien's *'lors'* indicates Arthurian times, although no one dare understand by it the sixth or any other specific previous century; it is a period which has no calendar dates, no British cultural background, not even, in this particular tale, a truly British place-name. As for Greece, it was evidently more remote, in Chrétien's mind, than the Britain of Arthur. There is such a marked difference between his descriptions of Alexander's setting out from Greece and his subsequent arrival in England that it is very difficult to avoid coming to the conclusion that the former was invented and the latter real. The ships in which Alexander and his companions were about to set out were loaded 'at the port' *'au port'* (231). Which port? Is it Athens or Constantinople? The following day the young prince and his retinue came 'to the sandy shore' *'el sablon'* (233) and we are now told that the port is 'beside the cliff' *'lez le faleise'* (238). When the anchors have been weighed,

7

the Emperor and Empress, together with the courtiers, climb to the top of 'the high ground bordering the water's edge' '*Lez la marine an un haut pui*' (259). All this is supposed to be a picture of a port at Athens or Constantinople but it reads very much like one of a seaport on the coastline of Normandy, which Chrétien probably knew well. That is why 'the port' in Greece is nameless and the scene of embarkation so general that it could have been witnessed anywhere and at any time.

As soon as the ships reach Britain, Chrétien suddenly becomes extraordinarily exact and knowledgeable. The place of disembarkation is no longer just 'a port' but the port 'under/below Southampton' '*desoz Hantone*' (269). He even states the time of Alexander's arrival: the ships dropped anchor in the early evening, '*antre vespres et none*' (270); and we are told that they had been at sea 'the whole of April and a part of May' '*En la mer furent tot Avril et une partie de Mai*' (266-7). These are singularly precise statements which call for further examination.

If 10 May be taken as a possible arrival date, in the light of '*une partie de Mai*', then sunrise at Southampton was at 4.24 a.m. and sunset at 7.42 p.m. Greenwich Mean Time. Chrétien has said that the ships dropped anchor 'between Vespers and None' but in view of what he says a few lines further on it is clear that he meant 'between None and Vespers' and that he wrote 'between Vespers and None' to accommodate the rhyme with 'Hantone' of the previous line, because None was between one and two in the afternoon and Vespers between five and six. It stands to reason that the ships would have come in on flood tide and high water. Normally there are only two high waters in a day but the tide in the Solent and Southampton Water is peculiar; it has a double high water morning and afternoon. Out of the full cycle of about twelve and a half hours the flood and high water period lasts nine hours, since the two high waters occur within approximately an hour and a half of each other. On 10 May these would come at 4.01 and 5.35 in the morning and 4.56 and 6.27 in the evening. As the flood and high water period lasted for nine hours, the Greeks would have come easily into port in the afternoon, any time between about two and half-past six.

These calculations have been made from modern tide-

8

tables[5] but they go a long way to support Chrétien's statements. In the complete line about None and Vespers he makes it clear that he was thinking of the regular diurnal time of None to Vespers, for he says the Greeks dropped anchor 'Un jor *antre vespres et none*' meaning None and Vespers of the same day, which could not be if it were 'Vespers and None'. Further confirmation is to be found in the following lines in which he says that the Greeks 'stayed the night' in the port 'under/below Southampton' '*Desoz Hantone se remainnent | La nuit*' (283-4). This repetition of 'desoz Hantone' is interesting. Chrétien has already said that Alexander and his friends came to port 'under/below Southampton', not 'to Southampton'. Such marked emphasis surely indicates a difference in location. Had he been writing solely from hearsay, it is unlikely that he would have particularised in this fashion. For him '*desoz Hantone*' carried a special meaning: it was not actually Southampton but somewhere near it. There is a nearby port which fits the description; it is Bitterne Manor, the site of Roman *Clausentum*. According to the *Victoria County History* its situation 'is curious and distinctive. Between the two suburbs of Southampton, called St Denys and Northam, the tidal estuary of the Itchen describes a curve which is a complete semi-circle; and on its eastern bank, inside the semi-circle and close to the river, stood *Clausentum*. . . On the north, west and south it faced the river and its walls were washed by the tide at high water.'[6] Southampton itself lies opposite. Since

5. In reply to my enquiries concerning this matter, I received the following courteous confirmation from Mr J. Graff, of the Tidal Computation Section of the Institute of Oceanographic Sciences: 'The reference you talk of in the twelfth century indeed implies that the writer was aware of the times of occurrence of high water at Southampton. This is not unusual, since the occurrence of high water follows a fairly regular pattern, recurring at intervals of about 12 hours, and the sequence of these times would be well known by mariners of the period. Calculation of these exact times would not have been possible but their approximate occurrence would have been fairly well established from rudimentary sums based on the passage of the moon, and its state of phase, at the location.'

6. *VCH: Hampshire and the Isle of Wight*, 1.332. See also 321, 330, 334.

this Roman site has been in continuous occupation from Anglo-Saxon times, it follows that there were landing-stages and habitations there in the twelfth century. It was evidently a well-known harbour facing the busier one of Southampton on the other side.

Details of this sort strongly suggest that Chrétien was well acquainted with the Southampton area and had often made the trip across the Channel to it; otherwise he would not have gone to such pains to pinpoint the time at which Alexander's ships arrived and the place at which they disembarked and stayed the night. To this display of detailed knowledge of locality may be added his telling description of the party after they had disembarked. A six week's voyage through the Mediterranean had left them white and tired; even the strongest and most healthy had become enfeebled:

> Li vaslet qui n'erent apris
> A sofrir meseise ne painne
> En mer, qui ne lor fu pas sainne,
> Orent longuement demoré
> Tant que tuit sont descoloré
> Et afebli furent et vain
> Tuit li plus fort et li plus sain. (272-8)

This, like Wace's description of the embarkation of Arthur at Southampton, bears all the marks of a picture founded on personal observation; they differ one from the other but each is individual.[7] Chrétien had evidently watched parties of travellers arriving on the quayside. It is also worthwhile remembering, in passing, that one of the streets in Southampton was and still is called French Street, because it was the street in which Norman-French merchants had settled since the time of the Conqueror, and would have been the place where visiting Frenchmen from across the Channel

7. *Brut*, ll.11175ff. A profitable comparison may be made between Chrétien's and Wace's descriptions. Wace, like Chrétien, appears to have known Southampton well but his long and detailed picture is concerned wholly with the embarkation of troops and the activities of the sailors as they hoist sail and weigh anchor. There is in it no characteristic which definitely associates it with Southampton. It could be a description of embarkation at any similar port, whereas Chrétien's localisation is unmistakable.

would naturally have congregated. As will be seen later on, Chrétien's acquaintance with special enclaves of French people in England was not confined to Southampton.

The Greek youths, unaccustomed to enduring the hardships of a long voyage, spent the night in the environs of Southampton and there regained their good spirits. At this point in his narrative Chrétien makes another happy blunder: the travellers enquire whether 'the king is in England' *'Si li rois est an Eingleterre'* (286). During the reign of Henry II, one of our most restless monarchs, this question was perpetually on people's tongues. Nothing could have been more contemporary and less Arthurian. It rings true; and Southampton was one of the ports he used when going to and coming from France. For example, he embarked there for France in August 1158, February 1165 and March 1166; he arrived there from Normandy in April 1157, January 1163, May 1165, July 1173, November 1185 and April 1186. These are only the crossings which happen to have been recorded in our documents.[8] It would have been the most natural thing in the world for a foreign visitor, especially one who was intending to go to court, to ascertain whether the king was then in England. The answer Alexander received was equally commonplace and contemporary: 'He is at Winchester' *'il est à Guincestre'* (287). The Greeks are then told, as all foreigners at Southampton would have been, that they could soon be at the royal palace if they rose early and took 'the main road' *'le droit chemin'* (290), which at that time was the old Roman road running from *Clausentum* to *Venta Belgarum*. This road, used throughout the Middle Ages, was still in use in 1900 and the main Southampton-Winchester road in our own time follows its course. Marie de France, in *Yonec* (358, 484), has the same phrase, *'le droit chemin'* to indicate the ancient but still used *Strata Julia* between Caerwent and Caerleon.

Next morning, at early dawn, which would have been about half-past four in early May, the Greeks set off and, as the journey was a matter of only twelve miles, they arrived at the palace of Winchester 'before it was the first hour of the day' *'Einçois qu'il fust prime de jor'* (298), meaning, 'before

8. R. W. Eyton, *Court, Household and Itinerary of King Henry II* (1878), *passim.*

11

the first hour after sunrise', which would have been about five to half-past, just when the court day was beginning. The huntsmen were always up before dawn preparing to take their masters into the forest at first light. It is surprising how accurate Chrétien is with regard to these small matters. His close attention to detail illustrates both his professional competence as a writer of fiction and his sound knowledge of the facts he is using.

Alexander and his companions dismounted at the foot of the outside stone staircase leading up to the great hall and, leaving their squires and horses in the courtyard, ascended the steps to present themselves to 'the best king who ever was and ever will be in the world'

> 'Devant le meillor roi del mont
> Qui onques fust ne ja mes soit.' (304-5)

In the next two lines Chrétien, with superb mastery, converts present into past by giving the name of Arthur to the king who was plainly, up to this point, the English reigning monarch:

> 'E quant li rois Artus les vois
> Molt li pleisent et abelissent' (305-6)

To anyone who knows Henry II's reputation, especially in 1173-4, the clever device is patent. He too, to his people and admirers, was, in the words of Jordan Fantosme, 'the best crowned king who ever lived, the most honourable, the most puissant in every land since the time of Moses'

> 'le mieldre curuné qui unkes fust en vie,
> le plus honurable e le plus cunquerant
> que fust en nule terre puis le tens Moysant.'[9]

To Marie de France he was 'the noble, valiant and courteous king who attracted all happiness to himself and in whose heart everything good found root.' Chrétien's description of the arrival of Alexander's party, their correct behaviour in removing their mantles and kneeling before the king, smacks too much of twelfth-century royal Winchester to be mistaken

9. *Chronique de la guerre entre les Anglois et les Ecossois*, ed. R. Howlett. *Chronicles of the Reigns of Stephen, Henry II and Richard I*, III, 2, 112-3, (RS, 1886).

for the 'ancient' court of King Arthur, but the transition from contemporary to Arthurian times is so smooth as virtually to escape notice. Gawain is introduced without hitch. He singles out Alexander to be his *compaignon*, his 'brother-in-arms'. This piece of information is dropped into the story so casually that it is not until later that the reason for it emerges.

After having brought Alexander and Gawain together, Chrétien turns again to the part of the plot which is of immediate importance, namely, the knighting of the Greek prince who has come to Britain for the sole purpose of being dubbed by King Arthur. He has, however, to prove his worth before he can obtain that honour. The way in which he does so is, once again, characteristic of Chrétien's ingenuity. In Geoffrey's *Historia* the fabulous King Arthur went back and forth to France via Southampton; so did Henry II. On his last journey Arthur had gone to war against the Emperor Lucius and had spent the winter after his victory over him in the 'land of the Allobroges', brought up to date by Wace as 'Burgundy'. From thence he was recalled by the treachery of Modred. Chrétien cleverly substitutes a contemporary parallel: 'King Arthur, at this time, wanted to cross over to Brittany'

> *'Li rois Artus an cel termine*
> *S'an vost an Bretaigne passer.'* (416-7)

No motive is given for Arthur's visit, but Henry II's frequent visits to Brittany were common knowledge. He was there, for political and military reasons in 1158, every year from 1166 to 1172, and again in 1187 and 1188. Chrétien's unexpressed assumption in *Cligès* is that for Arthur, who is, so to speak, the king of England in disguise, to want to pass over to Brittany was a matter needing no explanation.

What happens in England during Arthur's absence seems to have been created by Chrétien himself, with perhaps a faint echo of Modred's treachery in mind. It could have been inspired in part by the behaviour of some of Henry II's disaffected barons, notably Hugh Bigod, earl of Norfolk, Hugh, earl of Chester and Robert, earl of Leicester, the leading conspirators in the baronial uprising of 1172-3. Robert, the arch-traitor, was captured at Fornham St Geneviève in 1173.

The siege of Windsor castle, although fictitious, is depicted in terms of absolute reality as far as the place and the conduct of operations are concerned. There never has been an Earl of Windsor. The only reason why Chrétien created him, in the person of Angres, must be that he decided to set the scene for this important part of the story in an area which he himself knew well.

His timing of events will be seen to have been impeccable. Arthur had set out for Brittany in late spring and had remained there the whole of the summer. At the beginning of October messengers from London arrived with the news that Angres was preparing to seize the country and had stationed himself with his followers in London. Here Chrétien proves that he knows the normal route English royal messengers took to the Continent: which was from London, through Canterbury, to Dover:

> Vint uns messages devers Dovre
> De Londres et de Quantorbire (1046-7)

Just as Henry II, alarmed by the news the messengers brought to him in Rouen in 1173 of the rebellion of the earl of Leicester and the barons, had set out immediately to return to England, so Arthur set out at once to capture the traitor Angres, who, having pillaged London, had retreated to his castle at Windsor.

Chrétien now pauses to explain in extraordinary detail what Angres had been doing in the king's absence. During the whole of June, July and August he had been busy putting the castle in a fit state of defence; making palisades, ditches, drawbridges, trenches, gates, barriers, portcullises and a huge tower of dressed stone. It had not always been in such good repair. 'At that time,' he says, 'whatever it may be like now, it was not easy to be taken, for the traitor, once he had plotted his treachery, had closed it in with double walls and ditches and had had the walls buttressed with pointed stakes and a revêtement, so that they could not collapse inwards:

> A ce jor, comant qu'il soit ores,
> Qui le chastel volsist desfandre
> Ne fust mie legiers a prandre;
> Car li traitres le ferma,
> Des que la traison soucha,
> De dobles murs et de fossez

14

Et s'avoit les murs adossez
De pex aguz et de darciere
Qu'il ne cheissent par derriere. (1227-37)

For what reason does Chrétien add the parenthesis, 'whatever it may be like now'? What exactly does it mean? Does '*a ce jor*' refer to the misty Arthurian era or to an occasion when Chrétien himself had seen the castle? From what is known of the condition of Windsor castle in the twelfth century, it would seem that he had seen it when it was being or had been put in a state of good repair; that is, during the period 1169 to 1178. In 1153, at Wallingford, when the famous peace between Stephen and Henry of Anjou had been drawn up, the castle was placed in the custody of Richard de Lucy, Chief Justiciar. For the first seven years of Henry's reign no payments for any work done on the castle buildings have been recorded; but, later on, entries in the Pipe Rolls show that payments for work on the fabric and its defences totalled the considerable sum of £573 18s. 8d. This work, according to St John Hope, included the rebuilding of the royal lodgings, the enclosing of the castle within a wall of stone to replace the former palisades, the building of the great stone tower, the construction of four towers on the eastern curtain wall, four others on the south side, the completion of the defences by a continuation of the south wall up the slope leading to the great tower and, finally, another wall connecting the tower with the inner gate-house on the north side. There was also some work done on the walling-in of the middle and lower baileys. Broadly speaking, the repairs and additions made by Henry II covered almost the whole of the castle area; and, he adds:

'the completion of these works involved the substitution of walls and towers of masonry for the formidable timber palisades which had hitherto formed the defences and there can be little doubt that the new works closely followed the older lines. . . it is a matter of some interest to note how the course of the works . . . was influenced by the events of King Henry's reign. The quiet that marked its opening years is coincident with the building in a permanent form of the royal lodging for the king when he would visit his castle. The internal dissensions that began to trouble the kingdom in 1167 and 1168 are reflected at Windsor by the important defensive works undertaken from 1169 onwards; immediately after the King's return from his long stay in Normandy; and the rebellion of 1173 found the castle partly protected by its new defences which continued to be made stronger notwithstanding the peace in the autumn of 1174.'[10]

Is it unreasonable to suppose that Chrétien had seen the building and repairs being put into operation and that he had seem some of the old timber palisades being replaced by the new walls, and the great stone tower going up? Answer may be found in what follows immediately in the text. He goes on to describe correctly the situation of the castle: 'It sits on a high hill and below it runs the Thames.'

> Li chastiax sist en un pui haut
> Et par desoz li cort Tamise.' (1246-7)

Very trite, it may be argued. It was a commonplace in medieval fiction that castles stood on hills and were surrounded by rivers or moats. Chrétien, however, does not leave it at that; he adds something which cannot be mistaken for a writer's convention. When Arthur's host arrived at Windsor not enough of the day remained to allow them to do anything but find a suitable camping-ground and pitch tents:

> Ne ce jor ne lor lut antendre
> S'a logier et as trez tandre. (1249-50)

A remark of this sort could be passed over without query were it not for the fact that, in this context, it has particular point. Windsor, being twenty-five miles distant from London, was, in military terms, an extra long day's march. For an army plus baggage on the move, twenty miles was reckoned to be a reasonable march along good roads.[11] As far as I have been able to ascertain, the main West road out of London in the twelfth century was the King's Highway, the *Via Regia*, which ran from the Tower along present-day Oxford Street

10. W. H. St John Hope, *Windsor Castle; an Architectural History*, (1913), 17-18. See also R. R. Tighe and J. E. Davis, *Annals of Windsor* (1858), I, 31.

11. See Hilaire Belloc, *The Historic Thames* (1922 edition) 68-9 and 78.

to Tyburn (Marble Arch) and thence to Staines. It was part of the old Roman road from London to Silchester. At Staines a secondary road crossed the river and went north-west to Colnbrook. This road was on the south side of the Thames and led directly to the castle. In *Cligès* Arthur encamped on the north side of the river and therefore the route he took would have been, at some stage, different. According to Tighe and Davis the principal road and the 'most direct communication between London and Windsor' went through Slough and Eton. This would have brought Arthur and his forces onto the north side of the river. If he had taken the London to Staines road, he would have crossed the river at Staines and taken the normal secondary road towards Colnbrook; but, in order to get to the north bank he would have had to cross the Thames again at Datchet and so have arrived at Datchet Mead, the low-lying tract of land on the opposite side to Datchet village. The march to Staines, a distance of seventeen miles, would have been comparatively comfortable and easy, since the road was paved and good. The remaining eight miles of unpaved road, together with the crossing at Datchet, would have added to the difficulty of passage for troops and impedimenta and would have lengthened the time of the march. That is why Chrétien goes out of his way to explain why it was too late in the day for any military engagement, and that all the army could do was to find a suitable place on which to pitch camp. To this explanation he adds a further individual touch: the army encamped on a meadow on the north bank of the Thames. By this time the soldiers had pitched their green and vermilion tents, the sun was setting and its rays striking on the canvas. The reflection of the tents on the surface of the river glowed for 'more than a full great league':

> L'oz est sor Tamise logiee
> Tote la pree est herbergiee
> De paveillons verz et vermauz
> Es colors se fiert li solauz
> Si reflanboie la riviere
> Plus d'une grant liue pleniere. (1251-56)

Arthur's host and camp covered the whole of the meadow, 'Tote la pree', which is surely Datchet Mead, which, even in Shakespeare's time, was open field, beyond the ford at the

17

end of Datchet Lane where Falstaff was ducked in the river in *The Merry Wives of Windsor* (Act 3, Scene 5). Datchet Mead, being across the ford, was the obvious place for encampment. How correct Chrétien was in his observation can be judged from his *'Plus d'une grant liue pleniere'*, for Datchet Mead with its adjoining open fields, as it was in the twelfth century, would have covered an open stretch of between two and three miles east of Windsor and the league, in France, was and still is two and a half miles.[12] His sense of direction was also accurate. The tents would have caught the low, slanting beams of the sinking sun stretching across the meadow.

As one reads his description of the assault upon the castle, it becomes evident that his knowledge of the castle itself as well as of its surroundings was astonishingly exact. When Alexander saw some of Angres' men coming down arrogantly to disport themselves on the gravelly river-bank, *'par le gravier'*, incidentally, another accurate observation, for the Thames is on gravel, he and his companions 'from the other side' *'de l'autre part'*, decided to make a daring dash across the river to attack them. They launched themselves across 'the ford': *'El gué a un frois tuit s'esleissent'* (1307). This ford cannot be precisely located[13] but Chrétien goes on to explain (1471) that it was possible for Arthur's great army to move across the river without difficulty, since the Thames was desiccated, because there had been no rain for the whole of the summer. There had been such a prolonged dry spell that boats were stranded and fish lying dead on the river-bed. The level of the water was so low that the army was able to ford it at its shallowest part:

> *Et Tamise fu descreue*
> *Qu'il n'ot pleü de tot esté*
> *Que li poisson i furent mort*
> *Et les nes sechiees au port;*

12. A measure of distance which varied slightly from country to country. According to the OED, it is usually estimated at 'about 3 miles'.

13. In the eighteenth century there was a crossing called 'Old Ford' at the end of what is now River Street, just below the site of the bridge built in 1268. I am much indebted to Mr Michael H. H. Bayley, of Maidenhead, for this information and for detailed maps of old Windsor.

Si poist an passer a gué
La ou ele avoit le plus lé. (1467-72)

In medieval times the Thames was not banked as it is now; consequently, it fanned out over a wider area and was, for that reason, much shallower. At Windsor the bed was neither deep nor scoured. In a dry season the water-level would have been low; in drought conditions it would have been very low indeed. Contemporary chronicles provide some documentation of unusual weather during the twelfth century. There was a run of drought years from 1102 to 1149, the most extraordinary one being 1114. The second half of the century experienced several periods of excessive dryness, though none was so spectacular as the one of 1114. According to the *Annals of Tewkesbury* and the chronicle of Gervase of Canterbury, under the year 1157/8, there were earthquakes in many parts of England, and the Thames was so desiccated that it could be crossed dryshod at London: '*Eodem anno terrae motus factus est in pluribus locis per Angliam et fluvius Tamesia apud Londinium desiccata est ut siccis pedibus transiretur.*'[14] Inasmuch as Chrétien definitely states that the Thames was low because there had been no rain throughout the summer, it is unlikely that he had this 1157/8 desiccation in mind. He was not the kind of man to miss or omit the fact that the country had experienced earthquakes; his sense of the dramatic was too keen. There was also a phenomenal drought in Normandy in 1176/7, according to Robert de Torigni: '*In aestate et autumno fuit maxima siccitas unde in satio terrae messis et fenum ex majori parte periit et collectio missum et vindimiarum solito citius evenit.*' The same kind of weather may or may not have obtained over the south of England in that year; but Chrétien's remark has no reference to the phenomenal; it has the air of the casual about it; and again, he is right, for desiccation of the Thames was by no means rare. The clearest evidence I have so far gleaned comes from a much later source but it is, nevertheless, reliable if only because it is, like Chrétien's statement, a casual remark. The Thames was still unbanked in the seventeenth century and Dr Robert Plot, in *The Natural History of*

14. *Annales Monasterii de Theokesberia*; in *Annales Monastici* (RS, 1864) I, 48. *Gervase of Canterbury* (RS, 1879-80), 166.

Oxfordshire, written in 1677,[15] has this to say of the Thames: 'in dry times Barges do sometimes lie aground three Weeks or a Month or more, as we have had sad Experience in past Summers.' It was probably a dry summer and nothing more which caused the desiccation Chrétien describes and it is difficult not to believe that he was remembering what he had seen with his own eyes, as his subsequent account of the assault on the castle confirms.

After Arthur's army had forded the river, one part of it took up its position in '*la valee*', that is, the strip of low-lying ground immediately below the castle's north wall (Little or Home Park in Norden's map). The other climbed '*L'angarde*', the slope up to the castle itself. As might have been expected, the assault was a failure. It was labour lost, '*toz fu perduz li travauz*' (1500), for the simple reason that the army was trying to scale or batter down the impregnable wall on the cliff facing the Thames. Night brought an end to the fighting but no victory. Arthur therefore offered a gem-encrusted gold cup to any man, knight or mere infantryman, who could effect the ultimate capture of the castle.

During the respite which darkness brought, Angres and his council of war decided to put into practice the old, well-worn tactic of issuing out secretly by night to massacre the enemy while they were asleep. His men armed themselves and came out 'through an old postern toward the north-west' '*devers galerne / Par une anciene posterne*' (1665-6), in the part of the castle from which they thought the opposing army was least likely to fear attack:

> *D'icele part ou il cuidoient*
> *Que cil de l'ost mains se dotoient.*
> (MS BN. 1450)[16]

Details of this nature are unusual in a conventional description of a fictitious battle. Why should Chrétien specify a postern 'toward the north-west' and an 'old' postern at that, if he had not had a particular edifice in mind? A glance at the

---

15. The first edition was published in 1677. I have quoted from the second edition, published in Oxford in 1705 (239).

16. M. Micha has not included these lines in his edition of the poem (CFMA, 1965). They are to be found in MS Bibl. Nat. français 1450, and 1420.12560 'et le ms. de Turin.'

ground-plan of the castle will show that the north-west corner was on the side of the fortification from which attack would have been most difficult and least expected, since it was on the edge of the high chalk escarpment furthest away from the area in which Arthur's army had bivouacked. I cannot find any record of a postern in that part of the castle but this does not mean that Chrétien invented it; there may have been one there in his time. As will be seen in the ground-plan, there was one in the north wall of the lower bailey. Angres and his soldiers sallied forth from this far corner of the lower bailey with little fear of detection. They split up into detachments in order to surround the Arthurian troops and, had it not been for the moonlight reflected on their helmets and shields, they would have been able to slaughter Arthur's men as they slept. As it was, Arthur's soldiers were roused to arms and speedily mounted. Angres had divided his men into five companies: the first held their way 'toward the wood'; the second went 'along the bank of the river'; the third positioned themselves 'in the forest'; the fourth was 'in a narrow valley'; and the fifth spurred 'along the cutting in the cliff', because they intended to crack down swiftly on the tents and bring about instant surrender:

> Li un devers le bois se tindrent
> Li autre la riviere vindrent,
> Li tierz se mistrent anz el gal,
> La quarte furent an un val,
> Et la quinte bataile broche
> Lez la tranchiee d'une roche
> Qu'il se cuidoient de randon
> Parmi les trez metre a bandon.' (1709-16)

This means that four of the contingents advanced down the wooded slope leading from the lower or outer bailey, along the north front of the castle-wall facing the river and, most significant of all, through a cutting at the base of the cliff upon which the castle is built. Chrétien has described the site precisely. The chalk cliff, covered at that time with wooded slopes, rises abruptly to a height of about a hundred feet. The south and east sides of the castle were also, in his day, surrounded by forest (now Windsor Great Park) and it was in this 'gal' that the third detachment had taken up its position, thus preventing any possible means of escape for any of

21

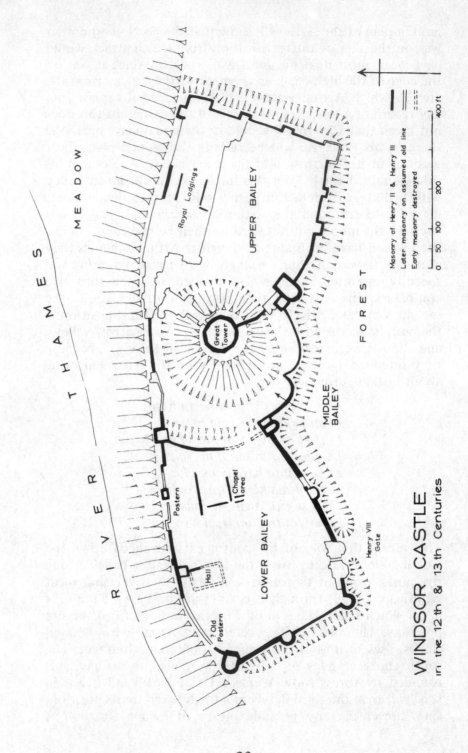

WINDSOR CASTLE
in the 12th & 13th Centuries

Masonry of Henry II & Henry III
Later masonry on assumed old line
Early masonry destroyed

0 50 100 200 400 ft

RIVER THAMES

MEADOW

FOREST

Royal Lodgings

UPPER BAILEY

Great Tower

MIDDLE BAILEY

Chapel area

Postern

Hall

? Old Postern

LOWER BAILEY

Henry VIII Gate

Arthur's men. The north-west slope, including the lower bailey, would have been well-defended by the new curtain-walls and towers, if they had been completed or else by the old pointed palisades. The great cliff was a natural barrier which not only provided the customary defence of a motte-and-bailey type castle but, since it ran down so steeply to the river, allowed an opposing army no more than a precarious foothold below. It was on this flat that Arthur's men were boxed in. Had they attempted to escape either by clambering up the slope or following a cliff path around the castle they would have been met by Angres' men in the forest behind. The alternative was to retreat across the Thames, which, of course, was not what the army of the heroic, invincible King Arthur could possibly do. His forces, although assailed on all sides, fought so valiantly and inflicted such losses on the enemy that Angres, despite the aid brought to him by his troops from four sides,

> De quatre pars voient venir
> Lor batailles por aus secorre, (1734-5)

left his standard on the field and, with his companions, began to sneak back to the castle along a hidden path on which they thought no one could see them, presumably a narrow track leading to the top of the cliff and around the wall of the lower bailey.

Alexander, who had spotted Angres and his companions retreating along this hidden path,

> une si coverte voie
> qu'il ne cuident que nus les voie, (1783-4)

decided to follow them with a band of picked men. It is worthwhile tracing their progress, for it will be seen that Chrétien knew the layout of the castle *within* the walls. They proceeded up the pathway along which Angres had gone, adopting on the way the ancient ruse of exchanging armour with some of the dead traitors. In this way they gained easy access into the castle, first into the lower bailey and then went on until they were inside the inner or upper bailey. The way in which Chrétien puts it proves yet again the accuracy of his knowledge. They went on, he says, until they had negotiated the three walls:

> 'Tant que les trois murs ont passez.' (1849)

Earlier, in v.1233, he had noted the *two* walls and ditches which could be seen from the outside; here he has correctly added the third wall or rampart which divided the tower from the two baileys. Finding Angres and his men unarmed, because they believed they were safe, Alexander and his companions braced themselves in their stirrups and charged. Angres, although he put up a good fight in the skirmish that followed, was outnumbered and retreated for safety to '*la tor*', the great tower, in which he was eventually overcome and captured.

Nothing in this description is false to the plan of the castle. The detailed account of the fighting after Angres had gained temporary safety in the tower provides additional evidence to strengthen the supposition that, when he was composing this episode, Chrétien had the actual castle at Windsor in his mind's eye. Twenty Greeks were detailed to block and guard the sole entrance to the tower, that is, the drawbridge and portcullis; and the remaining ten, including Alexander, made an assault on the doorway to the tower itself, to prevent Angres from closing it. Those of Angres's followers who still remained in the inner bailey rushed to attack the Greeks but they did not reach the gate to the middle bailey in time, '*Mes il n'i vendrent mie a tans*' (1971) and when they saw they had been shut out, they fell back and stayed where they were, since they could do nothing further:

> *Quant il voient qu'il sont forclos*
> *Si se remainnent a repos*
> *Car par assaut, ce voient bien*
> *N'i porroient forfeire rien.* (1975-8)

Chrétien uses the word '*porte*' for both the main gate and the door to the keep but his use of '*forclos*', inevitably reminding one of the noun '*forclose*', barrier, to describe how the mob of attackers were shut out of the main entrance to the keep, seems to imply the presence of drawbridge and portcullis. According to the plan of the old castle as it must have been in Chrétien's time, there must have been a drawbridge to span the deep, dry ditch around the motte on which the keep stood, since the keep was always the final defence and refuge. Its position, leading from the upper bailey, may be seen in the ground-plan.

If it be conceded from the foregoing analysis that Chrétien

knew Southampton, Winchester and Windsor from personal experience, when was he in this country? The nature of his references and descriptions suggests that he had some knowledge of our royal palaces, which, in turn, suggests that he may have been in some way or other acquainted with our royal household; not necessarily connected with it but in a position to know something of it. How this may have come about will be considered in the following section; for the moment it is sufficient to bear in mind that, having regard to what he says about the state of the castle and the desiccation of the Thames, he could have visited Windsor at any time between 1153 and 1174. Henry II and his queen, Eleanor, are known to have been with their Court at Windsor in 1155, 1157, 1158, 1163, 1164, 1170, 1174, 1176, 1177, 1179, 1184 and 1188. Since the drying-up of the Thames was not phenomenal, 1157/8 and 1176/7 need not be regarded as vitally important dates. It is much more likely that the years 1168-74 were the ones during which he may have been in England, because they were the ones in which he could have seen the repairs to the castle being carried out.

After the fall of Windsor castle, there is only one other precise reference to Alexander's adventures in Britain. When he and Soredamours leave, they set sail from Shoreham and this tallies with known historical fact. Shoreham was one of the regular ports of embarkation for the Continent. The Pipe Rolls contain innumerable references to it in relation to the shipment of the King's treasure as well as to the embarkation of members of the royal family and other notables.[17]

Much later in the story Alexander's son, Cligès, remembering his dying father's instructions, begs his uncle Alis for permission to go to '*Bretagne*' to see King Arthur and to measure his skill against that of his other uncle, Sir Gawain. He is duly transported, in two short sentences, not to Arthurian Britain but, once more, to twelfth-century England: 'and Cligès has passed over the sea and is come to Wallingford'

> *Et Cliges a la mer passee*
> *S'est a Galinguefort venuz.* (4530-1)

What has Wallingford to do with King Arthur? Why should Cligès go there? The answers to these questions lie not in

17. Eyton's *Itinerary* (n. 8 above), especially s.a. 1156, 1166 and 1167.

Arthurian legend but in Chrétien's knowledge of southern England.

In 1153 the long, miserable struggle between Stephen and the Empress Matilda came to an end, at Wallingford. Brian fitz Count, one of Matilda's dearest friends and staunchest supporters, was lord of the Honor of Wallingford and, during the war, until he died, had succeeded in keeping Stephen's forces at bay. In 1152 the garrison in Wallingford castle was so hard pressed that it sent a desperate message for aid to Matilda's son, duke Henry of Anjou, who was then in Normandy. He came to its relief and a truce was arranged at Wallingford, which finally resulted in the Treaty of Wallingford, under the terms of which Henry was made Stephen's heir. When he became king in the following year, he did not forget the part Wallingford had played in defending his mother's claim to the throne. In January 1155 he granted it a charter of freedom from tolls as a reward for the loyalty and great hardship its citizens had 'endured for me in the acquisition of my hereditary right in England': '... *pro servicio et labore magno quem pro me sustinuerunt in acquisitione hereditarii juris mei Anglie. . .*'[18]

Wallingford was an especially good town for Frenchmen visiting England. Before Henry's time it had already gained a reputation for being particularly hospitable to them. A hundred years before, Wigod, Sheriff of Oxford and Cupbearer to Edward the Confessor, had been a strong supporter of Duke William's claim to the English throne and after the victory at Hastings, when William, on his march from London, arrived with his troops at Wallingford, Wigod entertained him there. The town itself was founded on royal land. It was also one of the towns in which there had been a royal mint from at least the tenth century. According to the testimony provided by Domesday Book and Wallingford's roll of burgesses, numbers of Frenchmen held land, set up business and were resident there.[19] Like Southampton, it was a place

18. *Calendar of Charter Rolls*, II, 68. An inspeximus of the original charter.

19. My sincere thanks are due to Miss A. J. E. Arrowsmith, County Archivist, Berkshire, who provided me with a considerable number of French trade- and other surnames from the two earliest Wallingford Tallage Rolls (1226/7 and 1229).

where Frenchmen congregated.

That Cligès should have made straight for Wallingford need no longer cause surprise, although he was, according to the story Chrétien was telling, half-Greek, half-Arthurian Briton. In Chrétien's mind he was really a Frenchman, as v. 4934 eloquently proves. After he had performed so brilliantly in the tournament, Cligès was summoned to meet the king. He attired himself suitably for the great occasion: he went '*Vestuz a guise de François*', which would have been perfectly in keeping with the behaviour of a twelfth-century French gentleman lodging at Wallingford but doubtful for a Greek-Briton attending the court of King Arthur. This is one of the most delightful anachronisms in the story. Chrétien has momentarily forgotten he is supposed to be writing of Arthurian Britain; the England he knows and his national pride are too near the surface to be suppressed.

When he arrived in Wallingford, Cligès took a very expensive lodging and his servants kept their ears and eyes open for news to report to their master. They brought back information that the nobles of King Arthur were going to hold a tournament at which the king himself would be present; and the tournament field was to be 'in the open country below Oxford, which was near Wallingford' and it was going to last four days:

> Es plains devers Osenefort
> Qui prés ert de Galinguefort,
> Ensi ert anpris li estorz
> Qui devoit durer quatre jorz. (453-6)

The statement poses a problem. If Chrétien were using his knowledge of England here, he must have had a period other than that of Henry II in mind. In the lawless times of Stephen the barons held tournaments despite Papal and royal prohibitions. Henry II forbade the holding of tournaments in England, although his eldest son, Henry, with William Marshal as his tutor and protector, indulged in the sport in France. Marie de France, Chrétien's contemporary, took care to stage all the tournaments in her *lais* in France. It was not until 1194 that tournaments were legally allowed to be held in this country. A writ of Richard I, issued to the Archbishop of Canterbury on 22 August of that year, runs as follows: '*Sciatis nos concessisse quod torneamenta sint in Anglia in quinque placeis; inter Sarum & Wilton; inter Warewicke & Kenelingwrthe; inter Stamford & Warineford; inter Brakeleye & Mixbr'; inter Blie & Tykehill . . .'* A fee was demanded from the participants: every earl who wished to tourney at any of these places was to pay the king 20 marks, every baron, 10 marks, every knight holding land, 4 marks, and every landless knight, 2 marks; and *no foreigner* was allowed to take part: *'nullus extraneus ibi torneabit.'*[20]

Whether the stretch of open country between Oxford and Wallingford had been used as a tourneying-ground in Stephen's time is not known for certain but the evidence in Richard's writ suggests that it very probably had been and that Chrétien was sure of his facts. If he had not known the terrain he could have committed a bad blunder; tourneying-grounds had to be in level, open country. All those mentioned in the writ were so situated: Wilton-Salisbury in the broad valley of the Avon; Warwick-Kenilworth in the low-lying land of the Stratford Avon; Brackley-Mixbury at the west foot of the Northampton uplands; Blyth-Tickhill in the wide plain watered by the Trent, the Idle and their tributaries; and the Wallingford one, which concerns us, lying in the vale at the foot of the Chilterns and stretching westwards to the Vale of the White Horse, for I take the 'Stamford'[21] of the writ to be a copyist's error. If, as seems likely, it stands for 'Stanford', now called Stanford in the Vale, then the tourneying-ground in *Cligès* is exactly the one listed in the writ, for Stanford is about four miles west of Wallingford and three south-west of Oxford, 'below Oxford', as Chrétien accurately describes it.

20. Rymer's *Foedera*, I, 65.

21. N. Denholm-Young, ('The Tournament in the Thirteenth Century', *Studies in Medieval History presented to F. M. Powicke*, Oxford 1948) preferred to see the 'Stamford' of the writ as a village of that name 'in Suffolk, not far from Thetford and Bury, *not* Stamford in Lincolnshire' (244). Because this reading takes no account of the situation of 'Warineford', Lane Poole (*From Domesday Book to Magna Carta*, Oxford 1955) opted for the Stamford in Kesteven, Lincolnshire and took Warineford to be an error for Wansford (Bridge), 'a little south of Stamford on the Great North Road' (cp. Powicke, *King Henry III and the Lord Edward*, Oxford 1947) but it is very hard to accept the arbitrary change of Warineford to Wansford when Warineford is a regular medieval spelling for Wallingford.

28

If he knew so much about Windsor he probably knew the surrounding countryside and had learned that there used to be a tourneying-ground there in the recent past, when Stephen was king.

In order to provide himself with the three coloured suits of armour he required, Cligès sent three of his squires to London to purchase them and they returned to Wallingford with the black, green and vermilion suits carefully packed in new canvas. Such intimate details tend to carry conviction. Knowing from our records that it cost 3s for a suit of armour to be carried from London to Windsor, we can readily visualise not imaginary creatures bearing armour of mysterious import but real messengers coming home with their master's new mail-shirts, painted to protect them from rust and professionally packed by the armourer's men in London.

As soon as he had proved himself equal and sometimes superior to the classic Arthurian heroes, Cligès became very much a twelfth-century knight of the English royal household. He remained at court during the summer as if he were a regular knight of the king's household, accompanying the king throughout the length and breadth of the country as well as to France and Normandy:

> *Cliges avoec le roi demore*
> *Desi qu'au novel tans d'esté*
> *S'a par tote Bretaigne esté*
> *Et par France et par Normandie.* (5008-11)

The narrative reads as though Chrétien knew not only the land of southern England but the constitution of the English court and the itineraries of its indefatigable king. To take a random example: between Michaelmas 1165 and June 1166 Henry II and his court were at London, Winchester, Salisbury, Woodstock, Oxford, Porchester, Southampton, Falaise, Maine, Alençon, Angers, Le Mans, Chinon and Brittany.

Having completed this lively, realistic episode in the Thames valley, Chrétien returns to his Graeco-Byzantine tale. It is only when Cligès and Fenice have to flee for their lives from John's tower that the scene returns to England. Cligès naturally seeks his great-uncle's protection:

> *Au roi Artus son oncle en va*
> *Tant le quist qu'il le trova.* (6553-4)

29

Cligès' search for him sounds, once again, very like someone trying to find Henry II, who moved about England and France with such speed and unpredictability that anyone looking for him was hard put to catch up with him. Where Cligès caught up with King Arthur is tactfully not stated. One assumes that it was in England.

As soon as he has told his tale, the King issued a summons to muster all troops, not of 'Britain and Cornwall' but of England, Flanders, Normandy, France and Brittany, as well as of all the area up to the borders of Spain:

> *Tote Eingleterre et tote Flandres,*
> *Normandie, France et Bretaigne*
> *Et tot desi qu'as porz d'Espaigne.* (6582-4)

With the exception of Flanders, well-known for providing mercenaries, this is a list of the territories comprising the Angevin Empire. The year 1176/7 saw Henry II at the highest peak of his power. In view of the complete background to the plot of *Cligès*, it is interesting to note that entries in the Pipe Roll for that year prove that at the Court held at Westminster there were present ambassadors from the Byzantine Emperor, the Emperor of Germany, the Duke of Saxony, the Count of Flanders, and the Archbishop of Rheims. In this year also the kings of Castile and Navarre submitted a dispute between them to Henry II for arbitration.

The question of the general sources for Chrétien's Arthurian tales does not primarily concern us here but when we remember that Geoffrey of Monmouth was one of the witnesses to the Treaty of Wallingford in 1153; that in the summer of 1157 the sheriffs of London were charging the Exchequer for material provided by them to make Court dress for the Welsh hostages sent to the king by Owain Gwynedd;[22] that in July 1163 Henry II received homage from Rhys ap Gruffydd of South Wales and from Owain Gwynedd of North Wales; that in 1174 Emma, the king's beautiful half-sister, was given in marriage to Owain's son, Dafydd; that in 1177 in a general council held at Oxford, the princes of North and South Wales, together with several other Welsh princelings and nobles, swore oaths of fidelity to

22. *Pipe Roll 4 Henry II: 'Pro pannis obsidum Oeni Regis . . . 28s.'*

Henry,[23] then it would have been easy for a man of Chrétien's calling to have garnered much material for his stories had he been either present at the festivities or in the neighbourhoods of Wallingford, Windsor, Winchester, Oxford and London, because these princely Welshmen attended Court with their retinues of officials, squires, minstrels and interpreters. In like manner, stories of Arthur current in North Britain could have been among the items in the repertoires of the professional and amateur minstrels of Malcolm, King of the Scots, who paid homage to Henry in 1163. Again, in the spring of 1173 William the Lion and his brother, David, attended a Great Council held at Windsor castle; and on 31 May of the same year David received the accolade of knighthood from Henry. Such occasions invariably included festivities at which the domestic minstrels of all the lords present performed. There is neither indication nor proof that Chrétien ever visited Wales, but if he were about in England, particularly in the vicinity of the court, he would have had ample opportunity to stimulate his imagination with regard to things Celtic.

If the information given in the prologue to *Tyolet* can be trusted, collection and preservation of Celtic stories was simple and commonplace. It also implies that a corpus of Arthurian legend existed in Latin anterior to its appearance in the vernaculars. According to the author of this *lai*-story, Arthur's knights, on return from their adventures, recounted them at court next day. The learned clerics who were present noted them down, turned them into Latin and finally wrote down the finished product 'on parchment', because the time would come when the stories would be asked for again; and that is why, says the author, they are recited and retold now, having been turned from Latin into French:

> *Li preude clerc qui donc estoient*
> *totes escrire les fesoient;*
> *mises estoient en latin*
> *e en escrit em parchemin,*
> *por ce qu'encor tel tens seroit*
> *que l'en volentiers les orroit.*
> *Or sont dites et racontees*
> *de latin en romanz trovees.* (27-34)

23. *Roger of Hoveden*, (RS, 1868-71) II, 1334, s.a. 1177.

31

Apart from the fictitious Arthurian setting, which can be discounted since it belongs to the tale of Tyolet, this sounds sensible. Nothing could have been more ordinary than for a good story, told in the vernacular, to have been jotted down by an interested cleric and turned by him into a Latin version written down at leisure in polished and expanded form. The singers and reciters were the transmitters of stories by word of mouth, the clerics were the ones who were able to preserve them in writing; and Latin was their natural medium. It was not until the vernacular languages began to claim precedence over Latin as a literary medium that popular tales were written down in their original tongues. Furthermore, 'em parchemin' does not necessarily mean 'in a book'. The few manorial manuals left to us prove beyond question that both history and story were written on parchment rolls for private, domestic use.[24] Chrétien's Beauvais book was almost certain to have been in Latin and was, perhaps, no more than a summary of the Cligès story as it existed in the widely-popular compilation of moral tales, the *Marques de Rome*. Such a collection of *exempla* rather than a full-blooded story of secular, sensual love was likely to have been housed in a cathedral library. On the other hand, one can never be sure of medieval clerics' taste in fiction; they were adept at claiming to find moral instruction in quite unexpected places.

The 'Arthurian' episodes in *Cligès* stand out, because they give the impression that they were created out of personal observation and experience of England. How far he identified Arthurian Britain with the England of his time may be summed up in Alexander's dying words to his son: 'Dear son, Cligès, you will never know how well you stand in prowess and valour if you do not go to the court of King Arthur and prove yourself with the Britons and the English'

24. Not only 'chronicles of the realm' and romances but saints' lives also were written on rolls for private, household reading. The National Library of Wales has one such of 'the only known life of St Melor in Anglo-Norman'. It was apparently used by the nuns of Amesbury, where the abbey church was dedicated to SS Mary and Melor. The tale is distinctly localised: 'the events all occur in Britain, Cornwall and Devonshire'. For a comprehensive account of it and its contents, see *An Anglo-Norman Life of St Melor* by A. H. Diverres in the *Journal of the National Library of Wales*, XV, 1967, 168-76. See also p.47, no.37 below.

Biax filz Cliges, ja ne savras
Conuistre con bien tu vaudras
De proesce ne de vertu
Se a la cort le roi Artu
Ne te vas esprover einçois
Et as Bretons et as Einglois. (2565-70)

III

Whether Chrétien was in truth the author of *Guillaume d'Angleterre* has yet to be decided. The arguments so far put forward either in favour or against have depended largely upon how each scholar has reacted to the subject-matter and style of the poem. Internal evidence of this nature cannot be relied upon too heavily, because any work of art can mean something different to everyone who examines it. All that is certain is that the name of the author was 'Crestiens' but the odds are that there were not two well-known poets of that name boasting, at the same time, of their skill and concurrently producing work of high quality. Also, since Chrétien de Troyes was a man who found the sources for his tales in the narrative traditions of any country but his own, there could have been nothing unusual in his re-telling a story belonging to England; nor would the story as such have been beneath his notice, for, despite the fact that *Guillaume d'Angleterre* is not a tale of fashionable courtly life, it was a very popular one, judged worthy to be placed among an English king's treasures.

Of the two existing manuscripts of it, the one in the *Bibliothèque Nationale*, fr.375, dated 1288, finds its place among a collection of romances two of which are *Erec* and *Cligès*. The other manuscript is in England, in the library of St John's College, Cambridge, MS B9 (James 31).[25] It is a volume ornamented with finely executed miniatures and written throughout in the same hand, that of a brother of the Order of Preachers: '*Ce livre compila et fist uns freres de*

25. I am deeply indebted to Mr A. G. Lee, the Librarian of St John's College, who very kindly answered my queries concerning the manuscript and assured me that it was written throughout in one hand.

l'ordre des prescheors a la requeste dou roy de France Phelippe, en l'an de l'incarnacion Jhesu Crist 1279. Deo gracias.' Its contents are six religious items: Wace's *La Conception Nostre Dame*; fifteen signs of the end of the world; *La Vie Saint Paule*; a prose collection of Lives of the Saints; *La Somme le Rei*; and our poem, which carries the title, '*La Vie Saint Guillaume Roy d'Angleterre*'. The inescapable conclusion is that it was regarded as a saint's *Vita* and not a *roman*. Since the tale bears clear marks of having been based on well-known, ancient Byzantine tales such as the *Life of St Eustache/Placidas* and *Apollonius of Tyre*, it cannot, on this account, be maintained that Chrétien de Troyes would not have composed such a poem, because he did exactly that in his second half of *Cligès*.

The Dominican brother's collection was apparently intended for the use of the French king, a fact which in itself speaks for the worth and popularity of the poem; and there is evidence that another manuscript of it was in existence, also for the use of a king; this time, an English one, Edward I. Among the *Jocalia* or valuables housed in his Wardrobe in the year 1299/1300 there was, in the words of the recording clerk, *Unus liber de Romauntz qui incipit 'Crestiens se voet entremettre'*. Of its provenance nothing is known nor what subsequently happened to it but its presence among the king's books indicates that it was either a presentation copy or a handsome commissioned one worthy to be owned by the king and to be kept safely with a great Bible '*cum imaginibus deauratis*', two other Bibles, '*cum platis et imaginibus argenti*' and the Testament, in its leather case, upon which the nobles were required to swear their solemn oaths in the presence of the king and his justices. It is reasonable to assume that the clerk who wrote the *incipit* was copying what was under his eyes and that it was, therefore, not the manuscript now in St John's College Library, because the first line of this runs: '*Crestiens se uiaut antremestre*'; nor was it the same as the version in the Bibliothèque Nationale, which begins: '*Crestiens se veut entremettre*'. It must have been an independent copy. Therefore, between the years 1279 and 1299 three separate copies are known to have existed, two of them in royal hands and the third in a large collection of well-known tales.

The fact that Edward I's copy was catalogued and kept with the richly decorated Bibles suggests that the tale was taken to be, as its title in the St John's College manuscript states, a saint's *Vita*, a tale of a St William who had once been king of England. No such royal saint existed. He may be compared with the King Philippus[26] who was said by the author of the Icelandic *Saga af Tristram ok Isod* to have been ruling over England when Tristan and Iseult were alive. The only kings of England who were saints were Edmund and Edward. A contemporary of Chrétien who had retired to the abbey of St Edmund in the latter years of the twelfth century was Denis Piramus, poet and quondam courtier. He was occupying his declining years with writing a French poetic version of the life and martyrdom of the real English king-saint, St Edmund. According to Chrétien, the manuscript of the life of St William was to be found in the same abbey:

> *(Une estoire d'Engleterre)*
> *On troveroit a Saint Esmoing;*
> *Se nus en demande tesmoing*
> *La le voise querre s'il veut.* (15-17)

Juxtaposing *La Vie Seint Edmund le Rei* and *La Vie Saint Guillaume Roy d'Angleterre* raises a very large question-mark in the mind. There is no reference to St William in the abbey's records. He seems to be as spurious as the original tale of which he is the hero; yet, this tale, as Chrétien tells it, certainly appears to have been composed in East Anglia. It bears the marks of having been originally a minstrel production, adapted to suit the neighbourhood and religious house by which it was used. The framework of a saint's life

26. In this Icelandic version, which is generally taken to be an imperfect recollection of Brother Robert's *Tristrams saga ok Isöndar* (1266), it is Tristan's grandfather who is King of England and who is called Philippus. Paul Schach ('Some Observations on Tristram's Saga', *Saga-Book* XV, 1957-61, 118) says that 'Philippus was a popular royal name in the *lygisögur*; it is borne by kings in *Valdimars saga, Flórents saga* and *Barings saga*'. Since the reference in the *Saga af Tristram ok Isod* is to a king of England, there is the possibility that it conceals a vague folk-memory of the Emperor Marcus Julius Philippus (244-249 AD). A quadrilateral milestone was set up in Lancashire and dedicated to him. I am most grateful to Mr Stephen H. Penney, Keeper of Archaeology at the Lancaster City Council Museum for sending me a copy of the inscription on the milestone which is now housed in its collection.

was usually constructed out of some slight historical tradition and then overlaid with common legendary and/or pertinently local detail to suit the pilgrims and lay-folk who attended the abbeys on Feast days. That the Church and its monks were not at all averse to making use of and gaining profit from such supposedly religious tales is well attested. Perhaps the most apposite example is that provided by Ordericus Vitalis. What he has to say about the way in which he was able to record a reliable life of the notable St William of Gellone, the hero of the cycle of tales now known as those of *Guillaume d'Orange*, throws a certain amount of light on the problem Chrétien's tale presents. A monk of Winchester, Anthony by name, happened to stay for a very short time at the monastery of St Evroul. He had with him a copy of the *Vita* of St William of Gellone and showed it to Ordericus, who was delighted, because, he says, although there was a song about him commonly sung by minstrels, an authentic version, expertly edited by clerical scholars, 'is rightly to be preferred': *Vulgo canitur a ioculatoribus de illo cantilena sed iure preferenda est relatio autentica quae a religiosis doctoribus sollerter est edita.*[27] As Anthony was in a hurry to be off and because the winter's cold made writing with a quill impossible, Ordericus incised a shorthand summary of the tale on wax tablets and subsequently transferred an expanded version to parchment. Incidentally, this description confirms in large part, what the author of *Tyolet* said about the way in which Arthurian stories were originally recorded. Ordericus' remarks imply that minstrel versions of saints' lives were not unacceptable, a fact which is surely confirmed by the content and quality of many which have come down to us. They were composed for the edification and instruction (of a sort) of the general public and, of course, to provide daily bread for the minstrels. The monks, accepted them because they popularised the religious house concerned and brought in financial as well as spiritual rewards. It is interesting to find that *La Vie Saint Guillaume Roy d'Angleterre* figures in the same volume as *La Conception Nostre Dame*. Before he graduated to the composition of his *Roman de Rou* and *Brut*, Wace had been a professional reader and versifier of saints' lives for religious houses. In *La Conception Nostre Dame*,

27. *Historia Aecclesiastica*, lib.6, ed. M. Chibnall (1969), III, 219.

composed expressly to support the institution of a feast day for the Immaculate Conception (8 December), he tells us how poets like himself used to recite to the ordinary people who came to church on feast days the story of the particular saint whose festival was being celebrated:

> Quant nos la feste celebrons
> Droiz est que l'estoire en disons
> Bien fait la feste a celebrer
> Bien fait l'histoire a raconter,

a very natural and rational proceeding, considering that the vast majority of the worshippers could not read.

In all probability Chrétien's tale was based on the kind of saint's life out of which such recited narratives were made: a local legend laced with bits and pieces from other saints' lives; in this case Byzantine ones, very old and already widely-known. Chrétien has stamped it with his own brand of originality. Just as he fabricated the story of Alexander and Soredamors and placed the scenes of action in those parts of England he knew intimately, so he has taken from his bosom friend, Roger li Cointes, a tale apparently localised in East Anglia, and has transported the opening scenes to the West Country, more especially, Bristol. The result is not the kind of saint's life Ordericus would have called 'a religiosis doctoribus sollerter edita' but an attractive poetic narrative. He had not been commissioned to write it and Chrétien is always at his best and most original when he has a free hand with his material. He wrote up this none too easy story with the object of enhancing his reputation. In his introductory remarks he says he is going to busy himself with putting the tale into verse without adding or subtracting anything; but, although he intends to keep to the main theme, he is going to cut down the whole story to size by rejecting the subsidiary episodes. He is going to keep to the main road in order that he might finish the work as expeditiously as he can:

> La plus droite voie tenra
> Que il onques porra tenir,
> Si que tost puist a fin venir. (8-10)

These lines constitute his indictment of his original which must have been a prolix Latin prose tale, as most saints' lives are, full of digressions. The implied criticism is amply justified by analysis of the plot, which proved to be even more awkward to handle than the plot of the Graeco-Byzantine part of *Cligès*. As one reads his poem one gains an unmistakable impression that he is doing his best to trim what appears to have been a good but very unshapely story and to make its parts cohere. Every so often he falls back upon explanatory sentences such as: 'I have told you as much as I think necessary about the queen for the time being. It is now right and proper that you should know what became of the twins'. (1326-9); 'I have told you so much about the twins that I need not say any more. Let us begin again with the king. . .' (1946-10); 'but I must now return to the queen. . .' (2972-3). These are sure proofs of an unwieldy original. He encountered a similar difficulty, off and on, with the second part of *Cligès*: 'I must speak now of the maiden and Cligès' (2817-8); 'but I do not want to stop to speak of every detail (of their wedding); I want to return to Thessala and her potions' (3205-9). The canvas was too large, the scenes of action too widely separated, the groups of characters too tenuously related to allow even a professional writer like Chrétien to combine them into a completely smooth-running and self-evolving narrative.

The origin of the hero, William, is unknown but the names of the other characters in the story, with the exception of Lovel and Marin, seem to me to reveal the East Anglian original. Lovel's foster-father was called Gosselin (Jocelin) and Marin's, Foukier (Fulk). Both names are to be found among the names of witnesses to charters belonging to the abbey of Bury St Edmunds:[28] Gosselinus (No.134), Fulcher (No.135), Folcardus (No.144), Fulcherus (No.147) and Fulchardus (No.148). King William's wife is called Gratiene, a seemingly odd name for the consort of a king of England but the Bury charters contain a number of thought-provoking forenames for women in that area: Cassandra, Cecilia, Claricia, Leticia and Grecia. Gratiana does not occur but the presence of the others, together with Gosselin and Fulcher, all within the period 1148-1180, proves that, *in East Anglia at any rate*, it would not have been any more out of the ordinary for a man called William to have had a wife called

28. *Feudal Documents from the Abbey of Bury St Edmunds*, ed. D. C. Douglas (1932).

Gratiene than it was for a man called Roger to have had a wife called Cassandra: '*Rogerus Fader et uxor eius Cassandra*' (No.160). Lovel and Marin may be left aside, because they are self-explanatory according to the text and are obviously fictitious:

> *L'un fisent apeler Lovel*
> *Por le leu Lovel le clamerent.* (1334-5)
> *L'autre fisent Marin clamer*
> *Por çou qu'il fu trovés en mer.* (1339-40)

These are exceptions; the others do not appear to be French. Rodain(s), the name of Lovel's squire, is reminiscent of Old English *reodan*, 'of ruddy complexion'. The name given to Gratiene's aged, second husband appears in the manuscripts in a variety of garbled forms, indicating how unintelligible it was to French copyists: Gliolas, Guiot lays, Gleolais, Guiolas and Guioz blais. The most frequently used is Gleolais, which suggests Old English *gleawlic* (Middle English, *gleolic*; Anglian, *gleulic*, all with a soft -c), meaning 'wise, prudent, discerning'. Chrétien's description of the old man's character fits his name; he displayed great wisdom in settling the quarrel between the merchants as to who should have Gratiene and was a most excellent knight. (1053-5). The master of the ship in which William, alias Gui, sailed to Bristol and thence to Surclin, is called Therfes or Terfes, which might derive from Old English þ*earfest*, 'useful, necessary' or, since in both East Anglia and Galloway there were pockets of Scandinavians, from an Anglicised form of the Old Norse proper name, Þ*orfastr*.[29] All these names, as they appear in the text are plainly mutilated forms. It is impossible to be certain of their origin but since they seem to have an English ring in them they may help to support Chrétien's statement that the tale he received from Roger was '*une estoire d'Engleterre*'.

A review of the place-names is more convincing. King William and his queen, after they had decided to obey the heavenly commandment and go into exile, set out, not as would be expected of the King and Queen of England, from London or Winchester, but from, of all places, Bristol:

29. Attested on a bone comb-case, found in Lincoln. 'Thorfastr made me'.

Hors de Bristot grant aleure
U il avoient sejorné
S'ont vers une forest entré. (356-8)

Why Bristol? Was it in the original or did Chrétien alter this part of the story because he was familiar with Bristol and not Great Yarmouth? If so, the forest in which the royal pair hid themselves was Kingswood, which not only surrounded Bristol at that time but extended from the Avon westwards to the Severn, eastwards to the Cotswold Ridge and northwards to Wotton-under-Edge. Much later in the tale it transpires that the merchants who carried off Gratiene and the twins, respectively, set out from Great Yarmouth:

. . . sor mer a la veue
D'une foret de Gernemue. (1469-70)

The period of time during which the king and queen were wandering 'in the forest' until they came to the sea and found the cliff-cave in which Gratiene gave birth to the twins is expressed by Chrétien in a vague, non-commital

Ont tant de jor en jor alé
Que vera la mer s'ont avalé (441-2)

which was clever of him, because he seems here to be covering up the change from the forest around Bristol to that around Great Yarmouth, the latter being, no doubt, the correct place in the original. At the end of the story, when William returned to see the cave, Chrétien is careful not to mention exactly where it was. Bristol, by this time, is out of the picture. It cannot be that he placed the first scenes in Bristol simply because he wanted to have as background a trading port and a fair in order to bring William, disguised as Gui, back to it to find his hunting-horn; Great Yarmouth was also a notable and flourishing trading port and Henry I had granted an annual fair to Bury St Edmunds, the home of the story, in c.1124-9. Chrétien could just as well have begun his tale in the place where it ought to have been. In the later, abridged version of the tale, *Le Dit de Guillaume d'Angleterre*,[30] Bristol does not figure in the plot at all. William

30. The manuscript is in the British Library, Add. MSS 15, 606. A printed version from Parisian MSS was published by Francisque Michel in his *Chroniques Anglo-Normandes*, (Rouen, 1840), III,

remained in the forest as a hermit until a heavenly voice directed him to leave and seek the queen. He begged a passage on a merchant vessel and arrived in Spain; and when he was sent to England to a fair, he arrived at Dover. No place for the fair is indicated; presumably it was London. Thus the whole of William's sojourn in Galloway and with it his voyage to Bristol seems to have been Chrétien's idea. It is at odds with the rest of the East Anglian setting but, as will be seen later, there was a possible reason for it.

By comparison, the voyages of the queen and the twins are straightforward and, up to a point, logical. Gratiene, having been taken up the east coast from Great Yarmouth, is landed at a place called Surclin, Sorlinc (? for Sorclin) or Sollin, according to the various manuscript readings. In different parts of the narrative it appears as a *port* (1038), *pais* (1051), *vile* (2352) and *castel* (3126). It bordered on Caithness, the most northerly region in Scotland. All attempts to identify it have so far failed. The spellings of its name are obviously corrupt, although the suffix *-lin* is truly Gaelic and occurs in other Scottish place-names such as *Roslin, Leslyn* (c.1180), *Lescelin* (1219) and in the common noun, *dòirlinn*, 'an isthmus usually covered at high water'. As Chrétien uses it in the text it is by no means clear what or where Surclin was supposed to be other than that it was a seaport with a castle and township and was somewhere on the border of Caithness, but in the story its location was important, because it was to Caithness that Gosselin and Foukier had taken the twins in order that they could be eventually restored to their parents who were destined to meet at Surclin. In this part of the tale Chrétien seems to be depending heavily upon his original, while at the same time trying to fit his own additions and elaborations into the plot of the East Anglian one. Gosselin and Foukier were East Anglian merchants yet, to the reader's astonishment, their homes turn out to be in Caithness, a region of Britain so remote that even in the twelfth century it

173-211. The manuscript in the British Library is of the early fourteenth century and the poem is to be found on ff.140b, col.2 to 152. By this time King/Saint William was already being confused with William the Conqueror.

> *Le roy de qui la vie vous veil ramentevoir*
> *Il fu roy d'Engleterre et duc de Normendie.*

was regarded as the Ultima Thule of historians and story-tellers alike: *Erat autem deserta, nullo habitatore multis diebus inculta.* (Geoffrey of Monmouth, Lib. 4, cap. 17). It was largely populated by Norwegians and Vikings; so, too, was Galloway, where William was landed. Both regions stood for the deserted ends of the earth. Perhaps that is why William and his family were taken to them; they were the only wildernesses in the British Isles which could be regarded as substitutes for the Egyptian desert into which Placidas/Eustachius went. Chrétien has been careful not to particularise about either of them. When he needs to go into some detail, as, for instance, when he has to describe what happened immediately to his characters, he takes refuge in the safe, all-covering 'there':

at Surclin: *La prisent port, la sont remes,*
La fu ancree la nes. (1039-40)
at Caithness: *La u mestier portier les firent*
Si furent crestiien novel (1332-3)
at Galloway: *La a por serjant retenu*
Le rei uns borgois assases
Qui n'estoit pas juere as des. (988-90)

Compared with his accurate knowledge of Bristol this haziness is striking; it is another of the ruses Chrétien practises when he is hard put to be precise about something he does not know. He did the same thing in *Cligès*, in the second half of the story.

The difference between his treatment of local background in Scotland and England is high-lighted in the scenes in which William, as Gui de Galloway, returned to do business for his master in Bristol. It was his second trip from Galloway. The first had been wide-ranging, to fairs in Flanders, England, Provence and Gascony; 'and if', said his master, 'you go to traffic in those held at Bar, Provins or Troyes, you cannot fail to enrich yourself' (1963-8). Apart from the mention of his name in the prologue to *Erec et Enide*, this is the only specific reference Chrétien makes in the whole of his work to the place supposed to have been his native town. On the strength of it it has been suggested that the commodities in which William assured his master that he was very knowledge-able, namely, leather, alum, the plum-coloured *bresil* dye and '*gorges de woupil*', to which he added later on when in con-

42

versation with his nephew in Bristol, woad, wax and the scarlet dye, *graine*, were ones which Chrétien would have seen in the fairs at Troyes. This is unquestionably true, but they were common to all fairs, because they were staple commodities.[31] William's second voyage is considerably more circumscribed. On his outward journey he was to go to Puy and St Gilles and was to take his master's two sons with him to learn the trade. His first port of call, however, was to be England, because 'the high festival fair at Bristol would be taking place the following week'; that is, the week after his arrival in the port:

> Car a Bristot l'autre semaine
> Devoit estre la feste plaine. (2019-20)

Bristol's earliest fair was granted to the Priory of St James sometime between the 1150s and 1165 by William, earl of Gloucester, cousin of Henry II. It was held in Whitsun week. That is why Chrétien uses the word *feste* instead of *foire*. Earl William's charter confirming the grant uses the Latin equivalent: '. . . *concessi eidem ecclesie feriam quam habui apud Brist(olliam) in ebdomada pentecostes. . .*'[32] By con-

31. M. Wilmotte, 'Chrétien de Troyes et le conte de Guillaume d'Angleterre', *Romania*, 46, (1920), 1-38.

They were certainly marketed in Bristol, although evidence for it is late. See *The Marchants Avizo*, J(ohn) B(rowne), London, 1589, ed. Patrick McGrath (1957). It is surprising how closely details in this little book reflect the incidental remarks Chrétien makes concerning Gui's life with his master in Galloway. Several of the commodities mentioned in the letters, instructions, bills of lading etc. include those mentioned in *Guillaume d'Angleterre*. Like Gui, the merchant's factor was sent overseas to carry out business transactions and received commission for so doing. He took his master's son(s) with him to learn the trade; and he was expected to be, as Gui so patently was, a sober Christian. The factor was also advised not to indulge in gaming of any kind, 'especially dice or cards', which reminds one of Gui's master who '*n'estoit pas juere as des*' (991). It seems the habits and outlook of English merchants, particularly those in Bristol, had not changed over the centuries. Gui would have been judged an excellent 'marchant's factor' by these standards.

32. *Earldom of Gloucester Charters: The Charters and Clerical Administrations of the Earls and Countesses of Gloucester to AD 1217*, ed. R. B. Patterson (Oxford, 1973), 55.

trast, the fairs of Champagne were continuous throughout the year and each one lasted for about six weeks.[33] That Chrétien should deliberately state that Gui's master wanted him to attend the *feste* in *l'autre semaine* surely argues that he had the Whitsun Week Bristol Fair in mind.

It was necessary for William to go to Bristol, because it was to be at the Fair that he retrieved his old ivory hunting-horn from the youth who, twenty years before, had picked it up when the palace was being looted. There follows the account of how the citizens of Bristol told William's nephew, now King of England, that they had been struck by the likeness of the merchant Gui to his long-lost uncle, with the result that the king could not rest until he had met and talked with him. He tried to persuade him to give up his business: 'There are plenty of people to sell dyes, alum and wax: I have come to beg you to stay at my court. You shall be my steward; you shall have jurisdiction over the whole of the Thames country, from the river's source to its estuary. You shall eat every day at my court; and for those of your company whom you bring with you, hay and oats will be provided. You will be paid your wages at your departure; and of the customs and tolls which other merchants pay when they buy and sell, you shall be quit throughout my realm' (2192-2239).

Chrétien is back in twelfth-century England; more especially the part of England he knows well, namely, the West Country and the Thames Valley. In this long passage he provides evidence of his accurate knowledge of two particular aspects of the life of his time: the regulations applicable to those who were appointed to court service and the habit of granting freedom from customs and tolls to favoured individuals or communities. Both can be amply verified from the English Royal Household Ordinances[34] and general

33. At Bar, the fair began on the Wednesday before mid-Lent; at Provins, the first in May, the second in October; at Troyes, the first, the *foire chaude*, in June, the second, the *foire froide*, in October.

   See Henri Pirenne, *Histoire de Moyen Age*, (Paris, 1933), VIII, 90.

34. *A Collection of Ordinances and Regulations for the government of the Royal Household* (1799). See also M. Dominica Legge, 'John Pecham's Ierarchie', *Medium Aevum*, XI, 1934, 82.

charters. Similar but not quite the same regulations and exemptions obtained in France and other courts of Europe. The passage referred to above does not prove that Chrétien was drawing upon conditions that existed in England alone, yet they seem to have distinct and pointed relevance in their context, seeing that he was describing what an English king was offering a favoured subject, that is, high office in his court and judicial authority over the whole of the Thames valley. Comparison may be made with the status of Cligès at King Arthur's court and the benefits Henry II conferred upon Wallingford.

The importance of details such as these lies in the use Chrétien made of them in his narrative technique. They were part of his life in the sense that, as a creative writer, he was drawing upon his knowledge of the contemporary scene to enrich and invest with reality the work under his hand. There is no clue in *Guillaume d'Angleterre* as to the historical time[35] at which the action was supposed to have taken place. The time during which the king-saint lived was, like the time of King Arthur, dateless. Chrétien, therefore, was free to tell his story in his own way, which was, as in his Arthurian romances,

35. *La Vie de Saint Eustache* and *Guillaume d'Angleterre* are to be contrasted rather than compared. Placidas, supposedly living in Trajan's time (96-117 AD), although a good man, was a pagan and the Emperor's steward, whereas William is a Christian and a king. When the story opens Placidas and his wife already have two sons, the elder being four years old; but Gratiene gives birth to twins in the forest. A general resemblance in plot exists between the two tales but it is very slight. The similarities consist only in a man leaving home with his wife, losing her and his two children, one of whom is seized by and rescued from a wolf. The remainder is utterly different in both detail and treatment.

Skeat's note on Aelfric's version (*Aelfric's Lives of the Saints*, EETS 1900) is worth quoting here, because it emphasises Chrétien's treatment of the theme: 'The legend differs remarkably from the rest ... It has peculiar interest in being a secular and romantic story ... It is, in fact, the story of the knight, Placidas, appearing as Tale CX in the *Gesta Romanorum* (Swan's edition) which gives the story in full, with the sequel about the martyrdom. But in the English version of the *Gesta Romanorum* (ed. Heritage, EETS 1879) it appears in what was, perhaps, its original form, *without* that sequel: so that the story there ends happily, as it was clearly meant to do.'

45

the anachronistic one of presenting an unknown past in terms of the present; and so, we find him in all his tales proving that he was familiar with not only the details of aristocratic life but with those of bourgeois life as well; with tournaments, the army, the court and the fashionable attitude then prevailing toward the relationships between ladies and gentlemen; with ports, merchant-ships, fairs, the behaviour of business men and mariners; with the crudity of their manners and their all too savage treatment of strangers and beggars.

As soon as William had politely refused his nephew's offer and had set sail, presumably to continue his business trip to Puy and St Gilles, the background to the story fades once more into the mists of Pictland and Chrétien was again constrained to rely more heavily upon his original. We are told that the money he obtained from the sale of his prosaic, credible cargo at Bristol Fair enabled William to purchase one of oriental opulence: 'nothing more splendid could be found between Bristol and Aleppo': stuffs of royal purple, goldsmith work, quilts, sables, ermine pelisses, silver backgammon boards and golden chess-sets (2416-21). Even allowing for the well-attested inflow of rich Eastern imports into this country during the Middle Ages, this is an unreally large collection to have been amassed from the sale of a Galloway merchant's shipload of leather, wax, alum and dyes. Chrétien seems to be quoting from his 'estoire' but, with his customary skill, he makes good use of the borrowing, emphasising its splendour in order to make it a foil to the humbler objects on which Gratiene, now Milady of Surclin, was to fix her choice and which were to play such a crucial part in the development of the plot. These were the hunting-horn and the ring[36] on William's finger. For good measure he adds an aside calculated to keep the balance between the fantasy of fiction

36. There are several little weaknesses in plot in Chrétien's original. This is one of them. Up to this point there has been no mention of the queen's ring and how William came to be wearing it. *Le Dit de Guillaume d'Angleterre* supplies the necessary information. When Gratiene goes into labour in the forest,

> *Un anel qu'elle avoit osta d'entour son doy*
> *En soupirant forment en apella le rey*
> *Puis li a dit: 'Gardes cest anel de par mei'*
> (p.183. Michel, unfortunately, gives no line numbers.)

and earthy fact. The Steward of Customs, who considered his mistress idiotic to refuse William's offer of a hundred marks instead of the ring, to say nothing of her passing over the magnificent items in the cargo, made up his mind to get his own cut, on the quiet:

> Li senescaus de son paiage
> De son droit ne de sa constume
> N'i laissa vaillant une pume,
> Ains prist, se assener i pot.
> Le millor avoir qu'il i ot. (2504-8)

The same kind of hard-headed criticism was levelled at William in Bristol. His servant, when he was ordered to hand over the five shillings to the youth for the hunting-horn, blamed his master for making what he considered to be a very bad bargain: 'moult blasme au roi son marcie' (2117).

If, as appears likely, the scene of the original tale was laid in East Anglia, why should King William have been connected with Bristol? Was it Roger or Chrétien who substituted Bristol for Great Yarmouth? Was it because either or both knew Bristol well? Which brings us face to face with the key question: Who was Roger? Chrétien describes him in three ways: he was *Rogers li Cointes; Uns miens compains* and *Qui de maint prodome est acointes* (3309-10). At this distance in time the cognomen '*li Cointes*' is distressingly vague. *Cointes* could be used in numbers of contexts in varying ways; it could mean 'well-known' 'elegant' 'refined' 'educated' 'clever' 'courageous' 'spirited' and 'good-looking', all with an over-tone of 'exceptionally so'. A good example of its use in a context similar to that in *Guillaume d'Angleterre* occurs in three manorial manuals.[37] Alfred the Great is described in these words: *quointes hume e sage en totes choses*; and his

37. *Feudal Manuals of English History*, ed. Thomas Wright (1872). These are rare and valuable remnants of an aspect of minstrelsy for which there is, at present, little proof in terms of documentation. In the past they have been confused with genealogical rolls but they are summaries of English history, representing the kind of chronicle of events which did service in baronial and other households as reliable information and entertainment for the lord's family, household and guests. In all probability they formed the basic material for extempore minstrel composition.

son, Edward the Elder: *Iceste Edward le fiz Alvred ne fu pas si sage de lettruce cum sun pere mes il fu plus glorius e plus de real poer. Il fu cointes e de grant force.* The good qualities of our other kings are described with equal but different precision; it is only Alfred and his son who were '*cointes*'; they were regarded as being outstanding on account of their cleverness, skilful sovreign rule and military genius. They were out of the ordinary and it is in this sense, I think, that Chrétien and other people regarded Roger; he was an unusually able or clever man; he was uncommon.

The word *compains* bore a specialised meaning in the Middle Ages. It was not the equivalent of either *compagnon* or *ami*, although it included the general sense contained in both these words. Its modern French descendant is the colloquial *copain*, 'bosom friend', 'pal' or 'chum', originally meaning 'one with whom one eats one's bread'. Morphologically, it is the nominative of *compagnon* but in Chrétien's time, and probably long before, *compagnon* had become a new nominative, with a new meaning; a *compagnon* went about with one, in either work or play; he was the one who shared the same kind of life. The Latin equivalent was *socius*. In our Wardrobe Books minstrels who worked at court in pairs or groups or were blind and had to have a guide were called by the clerks *socii*, if the entries were being written in Latin, *compagnons*, if in French. A further, extended and highly specialised meaning was 'sworn companion-in-arms' 'blood brother', applied to two knights or soldiers who took an oath, confirmed by blood-letting, to be fighting companions on knightly adventures or even on mere escapades. *Compains* meant something quite other. Its Latin equivalent was *sodalis*, which meant, in the Middle Ages, 'boon companion' 'crony' or sometimes, in a very specialised sense, 'brother', meaning a member of a fraternity, society, guild, corporation or college. Jean de Balbi's *Catholicon*,[38] com-

---

38. Mario Roques, *Receuil General des Lexiques Français du Moyen Age*, II. *Lexiques Alphabetiques*, (Paris 1938), 384.

Concerning the meaning of *prodome*, Joinville (1224-1317), *Histoire de Saint Louis*, CIX, 306, para.559, gives the most contemporary definition. St Louis says: '*il a grant difference entre* preu home *et* preudome. *Car il a mainz preus homes chevaliers en la terre des crestiens et des Sarrazins, qui onques ne crurent Dieu*

piled c.1286, bears this out: *socius* is glossed *compagnon* and *sodalis, compains*. Throughout *Guillaume d'Angleterre* Chrétien draws the same distinction. Lovel and Marin, although they were unaware that they were twin brothers, were inseparable during their boyhood years; and when Lovel came across Marin, beaten and starving in the forest after they had left their foster-fathers, he leaped from his horse and cried out '*Compains!*' (1693-6). Later, after they had found their father, King William, and were, by this time, knights and companions-in-arms under the King of Caithness, Lovel explained that they had been bosom pals for a long time, '*Compains de boine compaignie*' (2842) and added 'We are sworn companions and brothers-in-arms', '*compagnon somes et frere*' (2845). Chrétien's usage, therefore, is well-defined. *Compains* meant something more intimate than *compagnon*; it implied a closer human relationship; so that his use of it when he applied it to Roger must have been deliberate; his '*Uns miens compains*' meant 'one of my bosom friends'.

Roger was acquainted with *maint prodome*. Here again one is faced with a word carrying a variety of meanings according to context. *Prodome* might mean a 'loyal' 'brave' 'gentlemanly' 'upright' 'worthy' or 'good (Christian) man'. In *Guillaume d'Angleterre* Chrétien uses it to describe the two merchants/burgesses, Gosselin and Foukier. When presenting them to his father Lovel said, 'Through these *preudomes* whom you see we are safe and sound':

> *Signeur, signeur, par ces preudomes*
> *Que ci veés, sains et sauf somes.* (3143-4)

ne sa Mere. Dont je vous di que Diex donne grant don et grant grace au chevalier crestien que il seuffre estre vaillant de cors, et que il seuffre en son servise en li gardant de pechié mortel, et celi qui ainsi se demeinne doit l'on appeler preudome, pour ce que ceste proesse li vient dou don Dieu. Et ceus de cui j'ai avant parlei puet l'on appeler preuz homes, pour ce que il sont preu de lour cors, et ne doutent Dieu ne pechié'.

'*Prud'homme était pour Joinville et pour saint Louis,*' says Sainte-Beuve (*Causeries du Lundi*, VIII, 528, (Paris 1853), '*ce qu'étaient le beau et le bon des Grecs, ce que sera le mot honnête homme au dix-septième siècle, un mot large et flottant qui revient sans cesse et dans lequel on faisait entrer le plus beaux sens.*'

Later on, when Queen Gratiene, in gratitude for their care of her sons, sought to reward them with rich robes and fur-lined pelisses, they made it perfectly plain that such genteel gifts were not at all to their taste: 'Milady, don't take us for dolts. If these robes were ours we'd make a jolly good bargain-exchange — fourteen sets of large lambskins and lengths of wollen cloth for each one' (3187-91). The queen smiled behind her fingertips at *le folie as deus vilains* (3198). *En vilain a moult fole beste* ejaculates Chrétien; yet, as far as he was concerned, Gosselin and Foukier could be both good, worthy men and crude, mercenary-minded tradesmen. It is the kind of wise judgement one comes to expect from him. By contrast, King William was called *moult preudom* by the youth who sold him the hunting-horn:

> '. . . li rois Guillaumes, mes sires,
> Qui fut moult preudom. . .' (2085-6)

One cannot but conclude that Roger li Cointes was acquainted with worthy men of every class, good, plain-mannered men and excellent gentlemen.

Sparse as they are, Chrétien's remarks about Roger help to throw light upon himself. Roger was either an Englishman or a Frenchman living in or well-acquainted with England. The fact that Cligès, on his arrival in England, had made straight for Wallingford makes one think that this town, so well-known to Frenchmen, would have been the place to which Chrétien, too, would have gravitated on his visits to this country. If he did, he could have met there a true Roger li Cointes, a man of outstanding ability; Roger de Wallingford, one of Henry II's favoured sergeants. Through friendship with him he could have come to learn those details about England and English life which find their way into his stories in rather surprising ways.

This Roger is a much less shadowy figure than Chrétien. As king's sergeant he was, *ipso facto*, a squire and member of the Royal Household. It is in this capacity that he first appears in our records. On 30 September 1156 Henry granted him, for his past services, the office of Usher of the Exchequer: *Sciatis quod ego dedi Rogero de Warenguefort servienti meo ministerium de Hostieria de Scaccario meo, pro servicio suo, cum omnibus pertinentiis eidem ministerio . . . idem Rogerus et haeredes sui habeant et teneant praedictum ministerium*

... bene et in pace et honorifice et libere et quiete sicut aliquis illud ... habuit tempore H(enrici) Regis avi mei ...[39]
The charter was issued at Pont Audemer in Normandy, where the king then was with the chief officers of his household. Roger was being rewarded for his good service in the past, a fact of some significance, because it implies that he, being a man of Wallingford, had been a supporter of Henry when he was Count of Anjou. That he was a sergeant proves that he was a military man and had probably been active in the heroic defence of Wallingford.

During the reign of Stephen the business of the Exchequer had become chaotic. After Henry's accession, Nigel, bishop of Ely, under the king's direction, undertook the reorganisation of the Treasury. Roger, who was to work under him, was evidently a man of ability, trustworthy and well-known to those about the king and to the king himself; a man equal to an exacting task. The important office of Usher of the Exchequer carried great responsibilities. The Usher 'kept the door' of the hall of the Exchequer and that of the Privy Chamber adjoining it; which meant that on his shoulders rested the onus of admitting or refusing to admit persons who came to do business there. In this capacity he was guardian of the records and of the safety of the Exchequer.[40] In addition to his duty at the Exchequer hall he had an outdoor one which could take him to all parts of the country: he had to transmit all summonses for the king's debts to the sheriffs throughout England. This he could do either in person or by a trusty servant. He received no wages but the gift of his office was a very valuable hereditary sergeanty attached to the manor of Aston Rowant in Oxfordshire, which was, interestingly enough, situated in the low-lying plain at the foot of the Chilterns containing the tournament field described in *Cligès*, just nine miles from Wallingford and Stanford.

Roger entered upon his new duties immediately, combining them at times with his ordinary duties as King's Sergeant, which latter often included the conveying of prisoners to and from their places of confinement. The Pipe

39. Thomas Madox, *History of the Exchequer* (1769), II, 272, fn.m.

40. On the whole subject, see the Introduction, by Sir Charles Johnson, to the *Dialogus de Scaccario* (1950).

Rolls testify to gifts and favours he received from the king and Nigel, the Treasurer, in 1156. In 1162 he was given money to cover his expenses when going over to Normandy to join the king. He died between 1165 and 1168, leaving a widow and two young sons. His descendants held his office in the Exchequer for at least a hundred years.[41]

The nature of his work entailed intimate knowledge of what went on at Court and the Exchequer. Had Chrétien known him as a *compains*, several things in *Erec et Enide, Cligès* and *Guillaume d'Angleterre* might be satisfactorily explained. On Christmas Day, the day of Erec's coronation, King Arthur's energy and generosity were romantically superb. Before 9.0 a.m. he had dubbed more than four hundred knights. The mantles he lavished on them and on all others present were made not of regulation serge or russet, trimmed with lamb's or squirrel's fur but of materials reserved for royal and aristocratic aspirants, velvet trimmed with vair and ermine, and embroidered with gold thread.[42] These were spilled out of the trunks in which they had been packed and were scattered everywhere for anyone to take what he wanted. Placed on a carpet in the middle of the courtyard were thirty large barrels of *esterlins blans*, for, adds Chrétien, 'at that time sterlings were current throughout the whole of Britain and had been since the time of Merlin' (6628-32), which is arrant nonsense. Sterlings were English money and 'sterlings blanch' assayed silver of full weight, the blanching being an operation peculiar to the English Exchequer.[43] Once again, Chrétien was seeing the dim time of King Arthur in terms of twelfth-century England. He was, in fact, describing King Arthur at Nantes as though he were Henry II, who, it will be remembered, kept Christmas with Prince Geoffrey at Nantes in 1169. The mental picture of the ancient British legendary king making a special journey from Tintagel, at

41. *Red Book of the Exchequer*, II, 659; *Pipe Roll*, 1155-58, 1159-60, 1160-61, 1161-2, 1164-5, 1166-7; and, for his wife and children, *Pipe Roll*, 1169-76; *Book of Fees*, I, 119; *Calendar of Inquisitions post Mortem*, I, No.763, II, No.528.

42. For details of adoubements and statutory liveries, see Constance Bullock-Davies, *Menestrellorum Multitudo* (Cardiff 1978), xx-xxv.

43. It was unknown in Normandy. See Johnson, *Dialogus de Scaccario*, xxii, xxxvii-xli.

Christmas-time, in order to have a Breton/Welsh vassal crowned 'King of Cardigan' and distributing *largesse* in the form of twelfth-century English money, is a mind-boggling anachronism, although one which can be thoroughly relished.

As bosom friend of Roger the Usher Chrétien might often have witnessed the packing and shipment of barrels of sterlings from Southampton, Shoreham, Dover and Bristol, ports from which 'the king's treasure' was regularly transported to the Continent, as the Pipe Rolls frequently record.[44] 'Treasure' did not consist entirely of coin; it included regalia, gold and silver plate and changes of raiment; and these, once accounted for, were safely locked up and not brought out again except when the king sent for them for his use. The Receipt, where the money from the sheriffs was paid in, was in Westminster but the Treasury, where it was stored, was at Winchester and was, like the later King's Wardrobe, a place in which all kinds of valuables were stocked: specie, bales of cloth and furs for courtiers' liveries, gold, parcel-gilt and silver cups and mantle-clasps for dispensing as gifts, especially to foreign envoys and favoured minstrels. There were also festive and ritual robes, crowns, diadems, coronets, jewels, reliquaries encrusted with precious stones, gold and silver-plated illuminated Bibles and other manuscripts, among which, as we have seen, was a copy of *Guillaume d'Angleterre* in 1299. With a friend like the Usher of the Exchequer Chrétien would have had the opportunity of seeing something of the English king's treasure and money at close quarters. He would also have felt safe in saying that sterlings 'blanch' had been current in Britain since the time of Merlin, because no one then knew, nor yet knows, either the correct etymology of 'sterling' nor exactly how long the coin had been current in England. Upon being asked, Roger could well have answered, and truly, that sterlings had been English coins for as long as anyone could remember. They and the term 'blanch' were certainly in use a hundred years before Chrétien's time.

Money was much in men's minds during the first years of Henry II's reign. Civil war, with turbulent, lawless barons coining their own money, had debased the coinage to such an extent that, in order to begin to put the nation once more on

44. For example, Eyton's *Itinerary*, 15, 55, 57, 91, 114, 173, 231.

its feet, a new one was imperative. Henry was prompt to deal with the situation. In 1157/8 a new sterling (silver penny) coinage was issued and blanching stepped up to enable payments of county ferms to be more uniform. If Chrétien had happened to be in England at the time he would have been able to have learned about it, particularly if his *compains* were Roger, the newly-appointed Usher. Also, among the thirty-three towns which housed royal mints were the ones he seems to have known well: London, Oxford, Winchester, Bristol, Bury St Edmunds and Wallingford.

One other detail connected with this matter ought to be mentioned. The blanched sterling which King Arthur had had delivered to Nantes arrived in thirty *muis* or barrels. This was how the King of England's money was packed when it was despatched from the Exchequer. Every barrel contained seven standard-sized Treasury sacks, each sack containing a hundred pounds' worth of sterlings, so that thirty barrels held £21,000 of twelfth-century currency. '*Molt fu li rois puissanz et larges*' (6605). Without doubt, King Arthur, as was to be expected of an ideal monarch, was being superlatively generous. Chrétien, while indulging in the romance-writer's use of hyperbole, was, at the same time, consciously or unconsciously, comparing the respective values of English and French money. When Henry II promised to pay his daughter-in-law, Margaret (daughter of the French king) £2,750 for her lands in the Vexin, he stipulated that the coin was to be 'of Anjou'; if she wanted it in English money, it was to be reckoned at fifty-four Angevin *sols* or shillings to one English mark (13s 4d). Therefore, in describing King Arthur's *largesse* in terms of surpassingly rich clothes and 'sterlings blanch' Chrétien appears to be emphasising King Arthur's generosity in terms of the King of England's financial strength.

The Treasury barrels, after they had been packed, checked and sealed, were loaded on a large waggon drawn by dray horses; and if the money were being sent across the Channel, it was stowed in the royal galley, *Esnecca*, and conveyed to its destination accompanied by a number of Treasury officials. The three major ports from which it was despatched were the three Chrétien mentions in *Cligès*: Southampton, Shoreham and Dover. To these Bristol can be added. In 1171, when Henry II was preparing to go over to Ireland, his money and other goods were sent there for trans-shipment.

There is no justification for assuming that, if he did visit England, Chrétien came only once. Channel-crossings were as frequent then as they are now. A Frenchman with friends in Southampton or Wallingford or London would have found no difficulty in making the passage as often as he wished. The kind of intimate knowledge that Chrétien displays of Southampton Water, the Thames valley, Windsor Castle, our ports, commodities, Bristol Fair, currency and perhaps the abbey of Bury St Edmunds makes it hard to believe that he had not gathered his information in person.

In M. Wilmotte's view,[45] the tense of the verb Chrétien uses when speaking of Roger indicates that he was dead at the time of the composition of *Guillaume d'Angleterre*:

> *La matere si me conta*
> *Uns miens compains, Rogers li Cointes.*
>
> (3308-9)

Roger de Wallingford died between 1165 and 1168. Chrétien, when describing the fortifications being built by Angres at Windsor castle, definitely gives the hearer/reader to understand that he is speaking of past time; that is, some time after 1169-71, when the extensive defensive work on the castle was being undertaken; the new coinage was issued in 1157/8; Bristol Fair was granted to the Priory of St James between 1150-65; the king was on his way to Bristol in 1171. If Chrétien visited this country, then, on the strength of these facts, he could have come at any time during the period 1157-71; and that period, up to 1165/8 was the time when Roger was Usher of the Exchequer.

The important feature of *Guillaume d'Angleterre* is the one that Chrétien takes care to establish: it was '*un estoire d'Engleterre*'. In what form Roger transmitted it to him no one knows, although the use of the verb *conter* seems to imply that it was passed to him by word of mouth. Did it contain all the ramblings Chrétien cut out? Or are we to understand from his

> *Une qui moult bien fait a croire*
> *Por çou que plaisans est et voire*

---

45. Wilmotte's edition, 125.

> On troveroit a Saint Esmoing;
> Se nus en demande tesmoing
> La le voise querre s'il veut (13-17),

that he himself had consulted the manuscript at Bury St Edmunds? If such had been the case, it could be postulated that Roger had come across the story in written form in the abbey, had given his friend a summary of it, had told him where he had found the book and that Chrétien had visited the abbey to read it just as he had visited the cathedral at Beauvais to read about Cligès and Fenice. Apparently the monks kept it among their books because it was a tale connected with their part of the country. For them it was a saint's life, from which much admirable moralising could be drawn. In its original form it no doubt contained a lot of good material for a sermon to be used on 2 November, the Feast Day of St Eustache. Aelfric had used the original Placidas/Eustachius legend for precisely this purpose two hundred years before.[46] The substitution of an English St William and a local background for a remotely eastern St Eustache of Trajan's time would have been all to the good as far as an English rural congregation were concerned; the moral import was the same. Traces of this original pious tale are quite evident in *Guillaume d'Angleterre*, some of them jutting out like stark pieces of bare bedrock.[47] Chrétien, by removing most of them elevated the tale into a realistic one of endurance, love, and fidelity between husband and wife, a favourite theme with him.

How could a tale so localised have engaged the interest of Roger and, through him, of Chrétien? One has no option but to assume that, in the first place, it appealed to them as a good story in its own right, for it undoubtedly is. As tellers of tales they would have appreciated its potential. Next, either Roger or Chrétien or both had personal knowledge of the abbey of St Edmunds. In Roger's case this can be fairly easily substantiated. He was bound to have been involved in

46. Ed. Skeat (1900).

47. Such as: the bright light, the thunder, the voice from Heaven; the advice of the chaplain; the eagle flying away with the purse; the long peroration on Covetousness; Gratiene's pseudo 'life-history' in order to preserve her chastity; the 'miracle' of the return of the purse.

both the preparations for and the actual occasion of Henry's and Eleanor's second crowning at the abbey in the May of 1157. As Usher of the Exchequer he would have dealt with the conveyance of the regalia, robes and money to the abbey, as king's sergeant he would have been in attendance upon the king; but there were other, more general ways of making contact with the abbey open to him. There were a number of highly-placed individuals connected with the court and royal households who held office in the abbey or were tenants of its lands.[48] Queen Eleanor's steward, Ralph de Hastings, was a relative and heir to Maurice de Windsor, the first great steward of the abbey. In 1166 another member of the same family, William de Hastings, the king's steward, was appointed by Henry II to be steward of the abbey. Henry's brother, William, then a young man in his twenties, held of the abbey the manor of Great Barton, in Suffolk, and after his death in 1164 his chamberlain became the chamberlain in the newly-established household of the king's eldest son, Henry, at that time nine years of age. The king's chamberlain, Warin fitz Gerold, who had been one of the witnesses to the charter granting Roger his ushership, bequeathed, shortly before his death in 1160/1, six librates of land to the abbey and the charter confirming it was signed at Wallingford.

What is interesting about these pieces of information is that between 1155 and 1164 the king's chamberlain, the king's steward, the queen's steward, the chamberlain of the king's brother and the chamberlain of the king's son were connected in one way and another with the abbey of Bury St Edmunds. Roger de Wallingford, as king's sergeant and usher of the Exchequer, would have been acquainted with all of them and in all probability went back and fore to the abbey on business for them. If he were Chrétien's Roger li Cointes, he was indeed 'de maint prodome acointes'.

Because nothing is known about Chrétien except what he himself tells us and nothing about Roger li Cointes except what Chrétien tells us about him, it is idle as well as foolish to pretend that the identity of either can be satisfactorily established until some indisputable facts are discovered. There is no evidence that Chrétien was ever in court or household service of royalty or of Marie de Champagne or of

48. Douglas, *Feudal Documents.*

Philip of Flanders. All indications, for what they are worth, are to the contrary. With the exception of just two of his tales, all his work, as far as we know, was produced independent of patronage. The detailed knowledge he displays of certain parts of English life and England leads one to surmise that he was a writer who lived and worked on the fringes of royal and aristocratic society in both France and England.

Because hundreds of men in the twelfth century were called Roger, I would not dream of presuming to say more than that Roger de Wallingford was the *kind of man* with whom a writer like Chrétien could easily have been associated: a favoured servant of the king, personally known to the queen, a military as well as a civil member of the royal household, a court squire holding important office and obviously a very able, clever man. With such a one as his *compains* Chrétien would have been in an excellent position to learn about England.

IV

The utmost one can do about Chrétien is to try to draw some acceptable conclusions as to his personality and his life from the way in which he has told his tales. The particular aspects of them which I have dealt with in this piece of research work deserves attention if only because of its oddity. Of all the countries mentioned in his various works, and they include France, Flanders, Germany, Spain and Greece, England is the one most fully described. Since he professed to be a teller of Celtic stories, it might reasonably have been expected that the place-names in them would have revealed some specific knowledge on his part of Celtic territory. There is none. His delineation of Wales, that is, the actual country, is non-existent; the places mentioned by name are purely literary, borrowed from Geoffrey's *Historia* or some other source, and consequently colourless and unconvincing. Of French towns he has very little to say, chiefly because the subject-matter of his tales has practically nothing to do with France. When all is said and done, he was, as a story-teller, a dealer in alien cultures. The way in which he has presented his tales of Arthur, has rendered them, as far as their Celtic backgrounds are concerned, at best indistinct, at worst un-recognisable; which seems strange for one who could have visited Brittany and Wales with ease. For a man whose awareness of locality was patently so sensitive and acute and whose gift for descriptive realistic detail cannot be gainsaid, the lack of identification of town and area in his re-telling of Celtic/Welsh stories points to total ignorance of the countries in which the action is supposed to be taking place, and complete dependence upon secondary sources, whether written or oral. Although the places he mentions bear authentic names, they are tenuous, pseudo and non-Welsh in the sense that they have not been given any marks of individual, actual existence. The ghostly feet of Erec, Enide, Yvain and Lancelot do not walk on *terra firma* as do the feet of Alexander and Cligès in Southampton, Winchester, Windsor and Wallingford. The Britain of Arthur was, for him, the England of Henry II. It is when he writes of England that his places come to life. He knows the time of high water at Southampton, how long it took to ride along the king's highway from Southampton to the royal palace of Winchester, what the day's marching distance was from London to Windsor, and from which ports the King's Messengers and Treasury officials embarked for the Continent. He can describe accurately the effects of a summer drought on the upper reaches of the Thames and can speak of London, that is, the old city area, as being situated where the Thames 'flows to its estuary', in other words, the Pool of London as it was in his day. He knows the lie of the land between Wallingford and Oxford, can remember on which bank of the Thames Windsor Castle stands, as well as the details of the castle's fortifications within and without the walls. He shows an intimate knowledge of English money, knows Bristol and its Whitsun Week Fair and possibly the abbey of Bury St Edmunds.

When an author is writing of what he knows in depth he is able to transmit to a reader an unmistakable impression of authenticity. Around these places in the south of England Chrétien has built up scenes which pulsate with life and which invoke immediate response in the minds of those who are familiar with them. They are not the kinds of scenes he draws in the land of Arthur. These are equally excellent in their own way, because the details in them have also been

drawn from contemporary life, but they could be seen anywhere, in France, Flanders, Brittany or in any part of feudal
Europe. The pictures he draws of England could not belong
anywhere else. It seems impossible to avoid coming to the conclusion that he knew the southern part of our country well.

In what capacity he came or how often we do not know
but from the range of his knowledge it is legitimate to deduce
that he was a man who had experienced life on various levels,
one whose appetite for life was keen and catholic, which is
what one expects from a first-class teller of tales. The value of
fiction lies not so much in the excellence of its literary devices
and theories as in its ability to create the illusion of truth.

Although Chrétien's identity may remain hidden forever,
his personality lies open for all to read. There will always be
innumerable and differing interpretations of his work. For
myself, I cannot but conclude from the evidence he gives of
the breadth of his experience, that he moved, as Chaucer did
later, between Court and town, between noble and burgess,
between tournament-field and market-place. Nor was the
Channel a hindrance to his alert and inquisitive mind. Apart
from his knowledge of France, which has to be taken for
granted, the country he appears to have known best and
which he so convincingly describes is England.

Among the collection of Berkshire charters in the Bodleian Library there is one (MS Ch.Berks.a.I. No.8) of a Master Christian of Wallingford, in which he made a grant in frank almoign of certain of his lands to the Priory of Holy Trinity in the town, in return for a daily corrody of food and drink for himself and one of his servants, together with stabling for his palfrey, and the right to live among the brothers '*in habitu scolaris*'. After his death, all his books, '*de diuina scriptura*', were to be given to the Priory 'to have for ever'.

The document is badly torn, especially on the right side and at the bottom, so that there is no indication of date; but we know from other sources that he was alive between c.1180 and 1201.

This is the kind of trick Fate often plays upon a researcher. Were it not that supplementary information about him is available, one could easily be led astray, imagining, with twists of wishful thinking, that this 'Crestiens' might possibly have been Chrétien; but he was not. Not only did he grant some of his lands to the Priory for his corrody and accommodation, but he stated in his charter that he had granted them for the health of his own soul and those of his ancestors, who had been living in Wallingford in the time of 'the King's grandfather', that is, Henry I. The *Curia Regis Rolls*, I, 413, 415, 430, 441, reveal that there had been a long-standing quarrel between him and Thomas Brancester, one of the King's Clerks. The squabble was about a mill at Brictmer, which both claimed as belonging to their respective prebends. When the case went before the King's Justices, in 1201, Crestien's brother, Alexander, attended as his attorney. In the *Curia Regis Rolls* he is called either 'Crestian' or 'Cristian'. According to the *Testa de Nevill*, 131 and the *Book of Fees*, Pt.I, 114, he apparently had two daughters, Christiana and Alvina, who gave five shoemakers' shops in Wallingford to the Priory in return for life corrodies.

Crestien – Alexander – Wallingford – '*in habitu scolaris*'. Without their historical background, fortunately preserved and to hand, how tempting these hints might have been. *Caveat scholasticus.*

II

THE *VERA HISTORIA DE MORTE ARTHURI* AND ITS PLACE IN ARTHURIAN TRADITION

Richard Barber

When Malory came to the end of his reworking of the story of Arthur's death as found in the stanzaic *Morte Arthur*, he clearly felt dissatisfied with what his chosen source had to tell him. For once, he put aside 'bokis that bene auctorysed' and inserted a substantial paragraph giving his own views. This hesitation on Malory's part is only the last in a long series of doubts and shadows surrounding Arthur's fate, and it is the purpose of this essay to look at the confused and often conflicting traditions of the death of Arthur, and in particular the unpublished account from Grays Inn MS 7.

Whoever chose the title *Le Morte Darthur* for Malory's work, whether it was Malory himself or Caxton, was right to do so. Just as Arthur is the focal point of the Arthurian romances, so Arthur's death is the focal point of Arthur's own personal story. In the earliest Welsh tradition, the brief entries in the *Annales Cambriae*, we learn of Arthur's triumph at Badon, and of his death in battle with Mordred. In early Welsh legend, Arthur is the centre of a glittering court, but at the same time:

anoeth bit bet y arthur

a line of verse which is translated as 'the world's wonder a grave for Arthur'.[1] The debate as to Arthur's survival was well-known in the early twelfth century, when Norman pilgrims in Cornwall found that the Cornish shared the

[1] Englyn 44 in 'The Black Book of Carmarthen "Stanzas of the Graves"', ed. Thomas Jones, *Proceedings of the British Academy 1967*, liii.127.

Bretons' belief that he would come back,[2] and Anglo-Norman chroniclers heard of ancient tales which fabled his return.[3]

Yet in Geoffrey of Monmouth there is hardly a trace of this potentially fascinating theme. He deals with Arthur's death in a single sentence:

'set et inclitus ille rex arthurus letaliter uulneratus qui illuc ad sananda uulnera sua in insulam auallonis euectus.'[4]

There is no ambiguity about 'mortally' (*letaliter*), for Geoffrey's artistic requirements in the *Historia Regum Britanniae* did not allow him to indulge in romantic possibilities. His portrait of Arthur is of a great warrior brutally cheated of victory at his hour of triumph by treachery at home, and within the briefest compass deprived of queen, kingdom and life itself. That Geoffrey's handling of his hero's death was deliberately abrupt is shown by the more extended version given in his *Vita Merlini*, when the same constraints of tragic effect did not apply: Taliesin, describing Avalon, speaks of Arthur's arrival as follows:

Illuc post bellum Camblani vulnere lesum
duximus Arcturum nos conducente Barintho,
equora cui fuerant et celi sydera nota.
Hoc rectore ratis cum principe venimus illuc,
et nos quo decuit Morgen suscepit honore,
inque suis talamis posuit super aurea regem
fulcra manique sibi detexit vulnus honesta
inspexitque diu, tandemque redire salutem
posse dibi dixit, si secum tempore longo
esset et ipsius vellet medicamine fungi.
Gaudentes igitur regem commisimus illi
et dedimus ventis redeundo vela secundis.

2. Hermann of Tournai, *De Miraculis Sanctae Mariae Lauduniensis*, ed. J. P. Migne, *Patrologia Latina*, clvi.983.

3. William of Malmesbury, *De rebus gestis regum Anglorum*, ed. W. Stubbs, RS (London 1889), ii.342.

4. Acton Griscom (ed.) *The Historia Regum Britanniae*, London 1929, 501:
    'Arthur himself, our renowned King, was mortally wounded, and was carried off to the Isle of Avalon, so that his wounds might be attended to.'

'It was there we took Arthur after the battle of Camlan, where he had been wounded, Barinthus was the steersman because of his knowledge of the seas and the stars of heaven. With him at the tiller of the ship, we arrived there with the prince; and Morgen received us with due honour. She put the king in her chamber on a golden bed, uncovered his wound with her noble hand and looked long at it. At length she said he could be cured if only he stayed with her a long while and accepted her treatment. We therefore happily committed the king to her care and spread our sails to favourable winds on our return journey.'[5]

Merlin, in reply, describes the tribulations of Britain since Arthur's death, and Taliesin exclaims:

> *'Ergo necesse foret populo transmittere quemdam*
> *et mandare duci festina nave redire,*
> *si jam convaluit, solitis ut viribus hostes*
> *arceat et cives antiqua pace reformet.'*

'Then the people must send someone to call on our leader to return in a fast ship. If he has recovered, he can exercise his old vigour to fend off the enemy and re-establish the nation in its old state of peace.'[6]

Merlin then goes back over the history of Britain before Arthur, describes Arthur's own reign, and ends:

> *Illic rex etiam letali vulnere lesus*
> *deseruit regnum, tecum per equora vectus*
> *ut predixisti, nimpharum venit ad aulam.*

'On that field also the king was mortally wounded and left the kingdom. As you have described, he sailed with you over the water and came to the palace of the nymphs.'[7]

Although the substance of these passages is well-known, the implications have not apparently, been discussed. Arthur

5. Geoffrey of Monmouth, *Life of Merlin: Vita Merlini*, ed. and tr. Basil Clarke (Cardiff 1973), ll.929-40.

6. *Vita Merlini*, ll.954-7.

7. *Vita Merlini*, ll.1122-4.

is quite clearly dead to ordinary life; Merlin describes him as *mortally* wounded. Avalon is an otherworld, from which, as in other Celtic stories, return is possible, but only under certain conditions. In Arthur's case, it seems from Taliesin's words that he can only return if his people need him. He is, however, not 'alive' in the orthodox sense, and much of the reticence as to his fate in later writers may be due to the fact that the belief in such an otherworld was not something of which the Church approved, and it was therefore wiser to leave the subject vague. Equally, there were political overtones to the belief in Arthur's return, overtones which may indeed have been the original reason for the development of the stories about Arthur in ninth- and tenth-century Wales, where it coincided with the emergence of the powerful rulers of Gwynedd, who almost succeeded in reuniting Wales and raised hopes of a reconquest of the lands lost to the English. These hopes were most clearly expressed in the tenth-century *Armes Prydein*, whose author speaks of driving the Saxons into the sea. A continuation of Gaimar's *Lestorie des Engles* says that the Welsh tell the Normans that they are bound to win in the end, because 'they will recover it through Arthur, and will take the whole country from the Roman people (i.e. Normans), and give the country its name back, calling it Britain again.'[8]

It has been plausibly argued that fears of a Welsh revival centred on the hope of Arthur's return lay behind the supposed discovery at Glastonbury in 1191 of the bodies of Arthur and Guinevere. Whatever the reasons — we can discount the remote possibility that the find was genuine — this discovery was widely accepted, and added a further complication to attitudes to Arthur's death. The one thing that it failed to do was to stamp out the idea of Arthur's return, which was by now far too firmly rooted in popular belief. We can now begin to classify the different approaches to Arthur's death after the twelfth century. Firstly, there is the main chronicle tradition, which follows Geoffrey in allowing some scope for doubt, mentioning the 'Breton hope' in passing. This appears in Wace and Layamon, but after the Glastonbury discoveries, chroniclers grew more wary: Peter Langtoft,

8. Quoted (French) in E. K. Chambers, *Arthur of Britain*, (reprinted Cambridge 1964), 109.

writing c.1307, says that he does not know whether Arthur is alive or not, and as late as 1514, Alain Bouchart's Breton chronicle keeps the tradition alive.[9]

Secondly, some chroniclers accepted the Glastonbury discovery, and rejected or ignored the 'Breton hope'. The most important of these are Robert of Gloucester and Robert Mannying of Brunne, as well as the popular prose *Brut*, which was among the most influential of all the chronicles. To this group belongs the alliterative *Morte Arthure*, where Arthur's burial at Glastonbury is described in very realistic, if suitably splendid, terms:

> He saide 'In manus' with mayne   one molde whare he
>   ligges,
> And thus passes his speryt,   and spekes he no more.
> The baronage of Bretayne thane,   beschopes and othire,
> Graythes them to Glaschenbery   with gloppynnande
>   hertes,
> To bery thare the bolde kynge   and brynge to the erthe,
> With all wirchipe and welthe,   that any wy scholde.
> Throly belles thay rynge   and Requiem syngys,
> Dosse messes and matyns   with mournande notes:
> Relygeous reveste   in theire riche copes,
> Pontyficalles and prelates   in precyouse wedys,
> Dukes and dusszeperis   in theire dule-cotes,
> Cowntasses knelande   and claspande theire handes,
> Ladys languessande   and lowrande to schewe;
> All was buskede in blake,   birdes and othire,
> That schewede at the sepulture   with sylande teris;
> Whas never so sorowfull a syghte   seen in theire tym!
>   Thus endis kyng Arthure,   as auctors alegges,
> That was of Ectores blude,   the kynge son of Troye,
> And of sir Pryamous, the prynce,   praysede in erthe;
> Fro thethyn broghte the Bretons   all his bolde eldyrs
> Into Bretayne the brode,   as the Bruytte tellys.[10]

However, even here the concept of Arthur's return makes an appearance. The poem survives only in the Thornton manuscript at Lincoln Cathedral, written about 1440, and in

9. R. H. Fletcher, *The Arthurian Material in the Chronicles*, (Studies and Notes, Philology and Literature X), Boston 1906, 202, 232.

10. *Morte Arthure*, ed. John Finlayson, 'York Medieval Texts' (London 1969), ll.4326-46.

this unique copy, the phrase 'Hic iacet Arthurus rex quondam rexque futurus' has been added. That this is an addition is clear from two things: firstly, the tone of the poem itself, with which such an idea is totally at variance, and, secondly, the placing of the additional line in the space which Robert Thornton usually left between the end of the poem and the *explicit*. On the other hand, the writing is very similar to that of Thornton himself, and it seems probabie that it was he who added it.[11]

If we accept that the Latin epitaph does not properly belong to the *Morte Arthure*, which was probably composed around 1360, its earliest appearance is in a short English rhyming chronicle on Arthur inserted in a Latin chronicle in the Red Book of Bath; the manuscript is slightly earlier than Thornton (being dated 1412-28), and the poem itself dates from the second half of the fourteenth century.[12] Surprisingly, in view of the fact that the manuscript was written not far from Glastonbury, the author claims that the epitaph was actually written on Arthur's tomb there, whereas both Leland and Adam of Domerham agree that the inscriptions were as follows:

> *Hic jacet Arthurus flos regum, gloria regni*
> *Quem mores, probitas commendant laude perenni*

and:

> *Arthuri jacet his conjux tumulata secunda*
> *Quae meruit coelos virtutum prole fecunda.*[13]

11. See *The Thornton Manuscript*, ed. in facsimile D. S. Brewer and A. E. B. Owen (London 1977). Erik Björkman in his edition of the poem (Heidelburg 1915, 11) says: 'Am Ende des Gedichts steht "Here endes Morte Arthure, written by Robert of Thornton", ausserdem von einer späteren Hand, "R. Thornton dictus qui scripsit sit benedictus. Amen." und von einer noch späteren "Hic jacet Arthurus, rex quondam rexque futurus".' Dr Brewer felt that Björkman's dating of the hand as later was unconvincing. See also William Matthews, *The Ill-framed Knight* (Berkeley and Los Angeles, 1966), 98-9.

12. Printed by F. J. Furnivall (without annotation) as *Arthur: a Short Sketch of His Life and History* . . . EETS OS 2, 1864. The dating of the MS is that of G. Guddat-Figge, *Catalogue of Manuscripts Containing Middle English Romances* (Munich 1976), p.232.

13. Quoted in Chambers, *Arthur of Britain*, 126.

If the first epitaph had been quoted at the end of *Morte Arthure*, it would have been entirely appropriate to the mood of the poem.

Thirdly, there is the example of the narrative of Arthur's death as found in French romance. *La Mort Le Roi Artu*, the last part of the Vulgate cycle, is the only such romance to deal with Arthur's death. A vast number of details are added, working from hints in the twelfth-century versions of his death, but the most important changes concern his last moments. The end of the battle of Camlan is marked by a single combat between Arthur and Mordred, a tradition found in a sub-group of the chronicles which otherwise follow Geoffrey of Monmouth, and which can be traced back to Henry of Huntingdon's summary of Geoffrey in his letter to Warinus:

> When Arthur saw that he could not retreat, he said, 'Friends, let us avenge our dead. I will now smite off the head of that traitor my nephew; after which death will be welcome.' So saying, he hewed a way through the host, seized Mordred in the midst of his men by the helmet, and severed his armored neck as if it had been a straw. In the act he himself received so many wounds that he fell . . .[14]

This fight between Arthur and Mordred occurs in about ten chronicles and in the alliterative *Morte Arthure*, and was therefore a relatively well-known tradition.[15] After this, however, the romance develops in new ways. In summary, the story continues as follows:

> Arthur and his two surviving companions Lucan and Girflet, go to a chapel beside the sea called the Black Chapel. 'Mass was sung there every day by a hermit who had his hut quite close by in a copse'. They spend the night in prayer; Lucan dies when he tries to lift Arthur. Arthur tells Girflet to dispose of Excalibur by throwing it into a lake by the sea-shore, which he does at the third time of asking. This is the signal for Morgan Le

14. *Chronicles of the Reigns of Stephen, Henry II and Richard I*, ed. Richard Howlett, RS, (London 1889), iv.65; translated in Fletcher, *Arthurian Material*, 120.

15. Fletcher, *Arthurian Material*, 120, n.

Fay to fetch Arthur, and Girflet watches her ship depart with the King for an unknown destination. He returns to the Black Chapel three days later to find two rich tombs, one being that of Lucan; on the other is written: 'Here lies King Arthur who through his valour conquered twelve kingdoms'. The hermit confirms that it is King Arthur who is buried there, saying that his body was brought by some unknown ladies, whom Girflet takes to be Morgan and her attendants.[16]

The substance of this account is reproduced in the stanzaic *Morte Arthure*, which Malory used as a source, though the details are somewhat simplified. On the other hand Bedivere replaces Girflet, Arthur's destination is clearly identified as Avalon, and the hermit does not know who is buried in the tomb (to which Bedivere comes the next day), saying only that the body was covered in wounds and brought by ladies.[17] In all these points, there seems to be a return to an earlier tradition, since Bedivere appears as Arthur's companion in the early Welsh sources. Avalon is associated with his death in Geoffrey, and the mystery about his fate is also in accordance with earlier accounts.

So far, our three groups of versions of Arthur's death represent a gradual expansion in different contexts of the basic story of the end of the last battle at Camlan. There is, however, a fourth approach, which is evidence that there were independent versions not represented in the 'authorised' tradition of Geoffrey of Monmouth or the Vulgate Cycle. This approach is found in a little known Latin prose text, titled *Vera Historia de Morte Arthuri*, preserved in a complete version in Gray's Inn MS 7, and in an abbreviated account incorporated in the *Chronicon de Monasterii de Hailes*.[18] Both

16. *La Mort Artu*, trans. James Cable as *The Death of King Arthur* (Harmondsworth 1971), 220-5.

17. *Le Mort Arthur*, ed. J. D. Bruce, EETS ES 88 (1903), 103-7.

18. Gray's Inn MS 7 appears in N. R. Ker, *Medieval Manuscripts in British Libraries: I London* (Oxford 1969), 435-7 and Pl.vii, and is briefly discussed by Lynette Muir in *BBSIA* xxi (1969), 109-110. The Hailes Chronicle entry was printed by R. H. Fletcher in *PMLA*, xviii (1903), 86-7, but apart from a brief paragraph in the same author's *Arthurian Material*, 188, seems to have gone unremarked since then.

have been partially printed, but until now their relationship has not been noticed. This *Vera Historia* gives precisely the detailed account of Arthur's death which is so conspicuously lacking before the Vulgate Cycle version, and offers the only account which includes a death-bed scene and account of his funeral. In short, it records a virtually independent version of a crucial part of the story, a sharp reminder that Arthurian tradition was not fixed and immutable but was open to the imaginative moulding of medieval writers as well as modern poets and novelists.

Of the two accounts, that in Gray's Inn MS 7 is by far the fullest; it is much more detailed for the first two-thirds of the text, and only in the last section, dealing with Arthur's burial, does the Hailes version substantially agree with it. In short, the Hailes version appears to be an abridgement, rather mechanical in style, of the Gray's Inn text. Internal evidence would tend to show that the Hailes chronicler was working from a better copy than Gray's Inn MS 7 itself, and that they may or may not share the faults of a common exemplar. So we can postulate the existence of at least three manuscripts containing this text. Rather than an eccentric, isolated re-working we are dealing with a text which evidently had a modest circulation. Further evidence of the circulation of this version may be provided by the epitaph already quoted, '*Hic iacet Arthurus rex qondam rexque futurus*'. The leonine rhymes in this hexameter are the same as those quoted by the Hailes chronicler in the poem at the end of his account of Arthur's death, which begins:

Rex fuit Arthurus: rex est post regna futurus.

This Hailes poem is at least fifty years earlier than the earliest possible date for the text of the English verse-chronicle *Arthur* in the Red Book of Bath, but it is of course possible that the epitaph was already in circulation in 1300, and that the Hailes poem merely provides the first trace of its existence.

The surviving manuscripts give few pointers to the origins of the text beyond that contained in the text itself. The statement that Avalon was in Gwynedd is otherwise quite unknown, and it is reasonable to assume that the text was produced there, particularly as there are one or two other details which imply local knowledge of that region. This is supported by the provenance of Gray's Inn MS 7, which is an

70

early fourteenth century English manuscript, formerly belonging to the Franciscan Friars at Chester, a small house founded in 1240:[19] it was given by 'frater W Gyn'. i.e. Gwyn. Gray's Inn has five other manuscripts from the same convent: of these three were given by the Franciscan writer Richard de Conway,[20] and it is not impossible that brother Gwyn was also from Conway. Interestingly, the only surviving book from Conway Abbey is a fifteenth century chronicle, also copied at Hailes at the end of a later chronicle from the latter.[21] Conway was a Cistercian house, so links with Hailes were more than probable; it is more surprising to find a link between Conway and the Franciscans at Chester, though the abbey may have had a business house at Chester, which was the administrative centre for North Wales.[22]

Furthermore, Conway or Aberconway was no ordinary abbey: it was founded by Llywelyn the Great in 1198, with a charter granting extraordinary privileges 'in itself an indication that it was Llywelyn's intention to make of Aberconway an exceptionally powerful establishment'.[23] Llywelyn himself and others of his line were buried there, and Aberconway quickly became the most important abbey in North Wales, ranking second only to Strata Florida, its mother house, in the whole of Wales. It was dedicated to the Virgin Mary, a point not without interest in view of the emphasis in the

19. Ker, *Medieval Manuscripts*, i.57.

20. Ker, *Medieval Manuscripts*, i.51, 56, 60 (MSS 1, 5, 12).

21. N. R. Ker, *Medieval Libraries of Great Britain* (London 1964), 54, 94; Rhys W. Hays, *The History of the Abbey of Aberconway 1186-1537* (Cardiff 1963), 144-5: '*The Register and Chronicle of Aberconway* runs from the reverse side of folio 40 to the reverse side of folio 65 of the manuscript, starting and ending in the middle of the page. The previous pages are taken up by a chronicle written at the Cistercian monastery of Hayles, in Gloucestershire, and since the Aberconway document is in the same hand, it too, in its present form, comes from Hayles, although there can be no doubt that it was originally compiled at Aberconway. Why a monk of Hayles should have cared to copy Aberconway material must remain a mystery.'

22. Hays, *Aberconway*, 110-2.

23. Hays, *Aberconway*, 23.

Vera Historia on Arthur's devotion to the Virgin: this is a tradition which goes back to the *Historia Brittonum*, but is rarely emphasised by later writers. Furthermore, the abbots are recorded as patrons of bards: there is a fourteenth-century ode to abbot Ieuan ap Rhys, and the abbey's chronicle contains a reference to the bards.[24] In 1284, the abbey had been moved to a new site to make way for Edward I's great fortress. Conway had been in English hands for only a year. I would suggest that these events might well account for the appearance about twenty years later in two English manuscripts of the full account of Arthur's death; and that the original manuscript came from Conway itself and was probably closely associated with the court of the last princes of Wales.

The content of the story and its style present a number of problems and there is little to help us in establishing the context in which the piece was written. It seems to be distinctly designed to continue Geoffrey's account of Arthur's reign, replacing the last paragraph which sums up the results of the battle, Arthur's fate and the handing over of the kingdom to Cador. The 'et cetera' at the end would indicate that the rest of Geoffrey's story follows. The most striking parts of the tale — the mysterious handsome young man with the poisoned lance, the chapel with the narrow entrance and the terrible mist and darkness which descended during the funeral — have their closest parallels in the native Welsh romances, such as the moment in the story of Pryderi where Pryderi and Rhiannon enter a magic *caer* or fortress and touch a marvellous golden bowl: they are rooted to the spot, unable to speak. 'And with that, as soon as it was night, lo, a peal of thunder over them, and a fall of mist, and thereupon the caer vanished, and away with them too.'[25] The spear is similar to

24. Hays, *Aberconway*, 153-4. The only other close link between either Chester or Hailes with North Wales was that between Chester and the small friary at Llanfaes on Anglesey, which was also in the custody of Worcester, and was founded by Llywelyn in 1245: but this is an unlikely source for a secular story.

25. *The Mabinogion*, tr. Gwyn and Thomas Jones (London 1974), 47; see also Martin Puhvel, 'Snow and Mist in *Sir Gawain . . .*', *Folklore*, 89 (1978), 224-8, who cites various Celtic examples, but no combination of storm and mist.

the poisoned spear with which Gronw Bebyr slew Llew Llaw Gyffes.[26] The adaptation of native Welsh story motives into Latin narrative (outside the pages of Geoffrey of Monmouth) is not common. The two Latin romances which derive more or less directly from Welsh material, the *Historia Meriadoci* and *De Ortu Walwanii* would therefore be *prima facie* candidates for common authorship with the *Vera Historia*. However, the differences between the extremely accomplished and ostentatiously learned style of the author of these romances and the naively simple rhetoric of the *Vera Historia* rules out this possibility.[27]

It seems, rather, that the piece is the work of a Welsh cleric with some knowledge of native tradition and a highly developed style of his own. The assertion that Avalon was in Gwynedd, and the account of Arthur's burial could almost be a counterblast to Glastonbury's claims, and there is a curious feature about the two bishops, Urien of Bangor and Urbegen of Glamorgan (i.e. Llandaff), who share the same name in different forms, in that the only bishop of that name in either diocese was Urien of Llandaff (bishop from 1107-1133) who seems to have been in charge of Bangor as well.[28] One last detail worthy of note is the precise and naturalistic description of the spear with which Arthur is fatally wounded: full grown elm is both twisted and knotted in the grain, but an elm sapling, such as a spear might be made of, will be true, and will also harden to a sharp tip if tempered in the way described. Giraldus Cambrensis remarks on the preference of the men of Gwynedd for the spear as a weapon: 'They use very long spears in this area. Just as the bow is the chief weapon in South Wales, so here in Gwynedd they prefer the spear. A cuirass of chain-mail offers no resistance to one of

26. *The Mabinogion*, 71.

27. I am most grateful to Dr Michael Lapidge for carrying out the necessary comparative study.

28. *Handbook of British Chronology*, ed. F. M. Powicke and E. B. Fryde (London 1961), 276, 274 n. The two names occur in a list of those at Arthur's court in Geoffrey of Monmouth (Bk ix. ch.12). Urien of Bangor is reputed to have been Geoffrey of Monmouth's uncle, according to one of the Welsh chronicles: see Fletcher, *Arthurian Material*, 44.

these lances when it is thrown a short distance as a javelin.'[29] Besides his knowledge of the tradition and customs of North Wales, the author seems to have been learned, to judge by his attempts at a rhetorical style.[30]

It is not impossible that the account of Arthur's death in the *Vera Historia* may have influenced the version in the French prose romance *La Mort Artu*: the chapel, the hermit and the mysteriously-appearing tomb are all common factors not found elsewhere. Equally, Malory's immediate source, the stanzaic *Morte Arthur*, may have drawn on lost traditions. The reversion in this poem to earlier names and episodes as noted above indicates a familiarity with material other than the Vulgate version, and there is one particular detail for which no source is known. Before the battle of Camlan, an adder comes out of a bush and stings a knight on the foot during a parley between Arthur and Mordred. He draws his sword to kill it: both sides suspect treason, and rush to the attack. The episode has been attributed to classical influence, and the issue is complicated rather than clarified by the appearance of the same events in a Spanish chronicle.[31] The Gray's Inn MS 7 version also mentions an adder in connection with Arthur's death, in that the fatal spear was poisoned with its venom. Might not both reflect an enigmatic remark about Arthur's death being caused by an adder (without specifying exactly in what way) in some Welsh verse which has not survived?

We may regard the traditions which Malory inherited as being in agreement as to Arthur's death; but it is important

29. Gerald of Wales, *The Journey through Wales and the Description of Wales*, tr. Lewis Thorpe (Harmondsworth 1978), 182.

30. Lynette Muir in *BBSIA* xxxi (1969), 109-110, points out a parallel with the death of Romulus in Livy's *Histories*. However, manuscripts of Livy were very rare at this period, and he does not seem to have been known in twelfth- or thirteenth-century Britain. The parallel exemplifies a generalised folklore motif rather than a specific borrowing.

31. Kirkland C. Jones, 'The Relationship Between the Versions of Arthur's Last Battle as They Appear in Malory and in the *Libro de las Generaciones*', *BBSIA* xxvi (1974), 197-205; Philip McCaffrey, 'The Adder at Malory's Battle of Salisbury: Sources, Symbols and Themes', *Tennessee Studies in Literature*, xxii (1977), 17-27.

to remember that even his main sources – the stanzaic *Morte Arthur*, the alliterative *Morte Arthure* and *La Mort Le Roi Artu* – had to be brought into reasonable harmony. Recent work on Malory begins to show him as something of an Arthurian expert: to have known these three works was in itself an achievement. The survival of the English poems in unique manuscripts is an indication that they were not particularly common: to have known one or other might be chance, but to know both looks like conscious research. This is borne out by the paragraph in Malory which follows the death of Arthur as given in the stanzaic *Morte Arthur*. Here he indulges in one of his very few complete departures from his main sources, disappointed – like the author of the Gray's Inn MS 7 account before him – at the lack of information about his hero's end:

> Thus of Arthur I fynde no more wrytten in bokis that been auctorysed, nothir more of the verry sertaynte of hys dethe harde I never rede . . .[32]

He goes on to give the names of the three queens in the barge, an insertion made for his own purposes.[33] He then reverts to a summary of what he has just related about Arthur's death and continues:

> Now more of the deth of kynge Arthur coude I never fynde, but that thes ladyes brought hym to hys grave, and such one was entyred there whych [the] ermyte bare wytnes that sometyme was Bysshop of Caunturbyry. But yet the ermyte knew nat in sertayne that he was veryly the body of [kyn]ge Arthur; for thys tale sir Bedwere, a knyght of the Table Ro[un]de, made hit to be wrytten.
> Yet som men say in many p[art]ys of Inglonde that kynge Arthure ys nat dede, but h[ad] by the wyll of oure Lorde Jesu into another place; and men say that he shall com agayne, and he shall wynne the Holy Crosse. Yet I woll nat say that hit shall be so, but rather I wolde sey: here in thys worlde he chaunged hys lyff. And

32. *Works*, 1242.

33. R. M. Lumiansky, 'Arthur's Final Companions in Malory's *Morte Darthur*', *Tulane Studies in English*, xi (1961), 5-19.

75

many men say that there ys wrytten uppon the tumbe thys: HIC IACET ARTHURUS, REX QUONDAM REXQUE FUTURUS.[32]

This indicates a wider reading than even his main sources. Firstly, Malory's use of the epitaph *'Rex quondam rexque futurus'* means that, because it seems to be interpolated in the Thornton manuscript, he either used that manuscript itself, or knew the source from which Thornton took it, either the verse chronicle *Arthur* or a source common to both Thornton and the latter. (*Arthur*, incidentally, has repeated references at the end to the 'Frensch boke' which are very reminiscent of Malory himself, but the author was alluding to a version of the *Brut* chronicle).

Secondly, none of his main sources mention the story of Arthur's survival, but the verse chronicle *Arthur* does include it, saying:

> *But for he skaped that batelle y-wys*
> *Bretouns and Cornysch sayeth thus*
> *'That he levyth yut parde*
> *And schalle come and be a kyng aye'.*[34]

The next piece of information appears to have no parallel: that he will win the Holy Cross at his return. I have found nothing in either chronicles or romances to suggest where this might come from, except in Malory himself: for the final words portray the four survivors, Bors, Ector, Blamour and Bleoberis going 'into the Holy lande' and doing 'many bat;aylles upon the myscreantes, or Turkes. And there they dyed upon a Good Fryday for Goddes sake.' Although Malory claims the authority of the 'French book' for this statement, no source has been found, and taken with the earlier remark, it looks on present evidence as though both are Malory's own additions.[35] Such additions are rare enough, and it may be that further research will show that Malory was more widely read in the Arthurian legends than we even now suspect. The Gray's Inn account of Arthur's death is an

34. *Arthur*, vv. 617-20.

35. *Works*, 1663. Matthews, *The Ill-framed Knight*, 99-100, suggests that Malory is imitating the endings of two of the Thornton romances, *Sir Perceval de Galles* and *Sir Degrevaunt*.

example, albeit an extreme one, of the variant traditions which were potentially available to him, and I would suggest that, quite apart from its intrinsic merits, it substantially alters our perception of the Arthurian traditions on which Malory drew by underlining the possibility of variations on the accepted versions.*

* Since writing the above, Dr Rosemary Morris has pointed out a possible Cornish folktale analogue to the poisoned spear episode. M. A. Courtney (*Folk-Lore Journal* V, 1887, p.87) says that Slaughter Bridge near Camelford was said to have been the scene of the last battle and that

'Arthur died here of a wound from a poisoned arrow shot by Mordred, and that after receiving his death-wound at Camelford, he was conveyed to Tintagel Castle, where, surrounded by his knights, he died. All the time he lay a-dying supernatural noises were heard in the castle, the sea and winds moaned, and their lamentations never ceased until our hero was buried at Glastonbury. Then, in the pauses of the solemn tolling of the funeral bells, sweet voices came from fairyland welcoming him there, from whence one day he will return and again be king of Cornwall.'

Courtney's tale seems to be an elaborated version of a story collected by Robert Hunt in 1863 (*Popular Romances of the West of England*, London 1881). The relevant passages (pp.303, 310) are:

The scarcity of traditions connected with King Arthur is not a little remarkable in Cornwall, where he is said to have been born, and where we believe him to have been killed. In the autumn of last year (1863) I visited Tintagel and Camelford. I sought with anxiety for some stories of the British king, but not one could be obtained. . .

At Slaughter Bridge I heard the story, but it did not sound like a tradition; the true native character was not in the narrative, – That in 824 the Cornish and Saxons fought so bloody a battle that the river ran with blood. On Slaughter Bridge Arthur is said to have killed his nephew Mordred, but that, previously to this fight, Mordred wounded his uncle with a poisoned sword, nearly in front of Worthyvale House.

I am doubtful whether these traditions are echoes of the *Vera Historia*, or derive from other stories about the death of a hero through a poisoned weapon, e.g. the death of Robin Hood.

77

III

AN EDITION OF THE *VERA HISTORIA DE MORTE ARTHURI*

Michael Lapidge

The *Vera Historia de Morte Arthuri* appears to survive in complete form in only one manuscript, London, Gray's Inn, MS 7, where it is found on fols. 60r-61r. The manuscript, which has been carefully catalogued by N. R. Ker,[1] is of unknown English origin but was subsequently in the possession of the Franciscan convent in Chester,[2] and is datable on palaeographical grounds to the very beginning of the fourteenth century (s. xiv in). The text in question has never been printed. However, in cataloguing the manuscript, Ker had occasion to transcribe the first 93 lines (as printed below = fol. 60r-v); his transcription is generally very accurate,[3] and incorporates some excellent conjectures by R. W. Hunt.[4] The text printed below is of necessity based primarily on this

1. N. R. Ker, *Medieval Manuscripts in British Libraries: I London* (Oxford 1969), 56-7.

2. N. R. Ker, *Medieval Libraries of Great Britain*, 2nd edn. (London 1964), 50.

3. *Medieval Manuscripts in British Libraries: I*, 435-6. There are a few minor slips: e.g. *accersiunt* for *accersiuit* in 1.14, *conterritus* for *concitus* in 1.30, *recompesat* for *recompensat* in 1.58, *uictoria* for *uictorie* in 1.71, and *sortita* for *sortitus* in 1.89.

4. Hunt's conjecture *ueneno* for MS *ueo* in 1.25 is confirmed by the abbreviated text in the *Chronicon* of Hailes. Another conjecture (*conamine* in 1.92), though it cannot be confirmed by the Hailes manuscript (which omits the passage in question) is almost certainly correct.

manuscript,[5] but (as the apparatus will indicate) the copy is very far from being an accurate one.

Some index to the accuracy of the copy in the Gray's Inn manuscript is provided by an abbreviated version of the same text which has been incorporated into the (unprinted) *Chronicon Monasterii de Hales*.[6] Hales, or Heyles (now Hailes in Gloucestershire, about 10 miles north-east of Cheltenham) was a Cistercian abbey whose principal records — the *Chronicon* and *Annales* of the monastery — are preserved in London, British Library, MS Cotton Cleopatra D.III. Like many Cottonian manuscripts, Cleopatra D.III is a composite codex, but the first 73 folios are evidently of Hailes origin. These folios consist in eight quires,[7] the first six containing the so-called *Chronicon*, the last two the *Annales*.[8] The *Chronicon* was written continuously up to the year 1301 (fol. 52r); thereafter are found entries in different hands for subsequent years up to 1314 (fol. 56v), when entries cease altogether. The remainder of the quire is blank. Similarly, entries were made in the *Annales* up until 1295 (fol. 72r); although the manuscript was ruled to incorporate entries up to 1319, none were entered. In other words, this manuscript provides evidence of some brisk historical activity at Hailes at the very end of the thirteenth century; this activity then peters out and finally ceases after 1314. What is of interest to us is that the compiler of the *Chronicon*, writing in 1301 or just before, saw fit to incorporate an abbreviated version of the *Vera Historia* into his account of early kings of Britain. This abbreviated text is found on fols. 7v-8r of Cleopatra D.III.[9]

5. I am grateful to Mr P. C. Beddingham, Librarian of Gray's Inn, for kindnesses during my consultation of the manuscript (many years ago), and to Richard Barber who supplied me with some excellent photographs of the folios in question.

6. See T. D. Hardy, *Descriptive Catalogue of Materials relating to the History of Great Britain*, 3 vols. RS (London 1862-71), III, 352.

7. The collation is: for the *Chronicon* I^{12}-V^{12}, VI^8 (8 canc, 10 canc); and for the *Annales* VII^{12}, VIII^4.

8. Printed in the *Monumenta Germaniae Historica, Scriptores* XVI, 482-3.

9. The manuscript has been partially refoliated (but only as far as fol. 13); for convenience I follow the older foliation. In the new foliation, the abbreviated *Vera Historia de Morte Arthuri* is found on fols 9v-10r.

It was noticed early this century by R. H. Fletcher, and printed by him among a collection of Arthurian fragments.[10] However, Fletcher was unaware of the Gray's Inn manuscript, and his transcription of Cleopatra D.III is so slovenly that it reduces the text to nonsense. Nevertheless, this abbreviated version, copied at Hailes at the very beginning of the fourteenth century, is an important witness to the text of the *Vera Historia* at those points where it is extant.

There need be no doubt that the version in the *Chronicon* of Hailes is in fact an abbreviation of the *Vera Historia*. Where it is extant it agrees with the Gray's Inn text *verbatim*. A comparison of the two texts indicates that the Hailes chronicler simply deleted entire sentences of the text in order to effect his abbreviation (as can be seen from the apparatus, below). It is also clear that he was not using the Gray's Inn manuscript as his base text: the two manuscripts are virtually contemporary, and there are numerous errors in the Gray's Inn text (as well as one significant lacuna) that are avoided by the Hailes chronicler. The manuscripts are therefore independent witnesses to the text, and where they disagree, their several readings must be adjudicated on merit.

The date and origin of the *Vera Historia* remain in doubt. It is clearly later in date than Geoffrey of Monmouth (hence *post* 1136), to judge from the reference to Modred as Arthur's betrayer *and* nephew in ll. 2-3 (cf. *Historia Regum Britanniae* X.2). The manuscripts suggest a *terminus ante quem* in the late thirteenth century. The fact that the provenance of each manuscript is a monastery on the Welsh march, and the fact that the incidents described take place in Gwynedd (*Venodotia*) conspire to suggest a Welsh origin for the work. Similarly, the fact that St David, *arch*bishop of Menevia (St David's), is mentioned in the text may point to the period in the very early thirteenth century (before 1203) when an earlier controversy about the metropolitan status of St David's was revived by the redoubtable Gerald

10. R. H. Fletcher, 'Some Arthurian Fragments from Fourteenth-Century Chronicles I: The Account of the Death of King Arthur in the *Cronicon Monasterii de Hales*', *PMLA* XVIII (1903), 84-89.

of Wales (Giraldus Cambrensis).[11] Questions such as these await systematic investigation by students of Arthur and of medieval Welsh history.

11. See J. E. Lloyd, *History of Wales from the Earliest Times to the Edwardian Conquest*, 3rd edn. (London 1939), 623-31. Perhaps significantly, the English archbishop who officiates at Arthur's funeral is from London, not Canterbury, the arch-rival of St David's (of course, on the other hand, it would have been anachronistic to speak of an archbishop of Canterbury in a period before the advent of St Augustine). The *Vera Historia* could have been written at any time such controversies were remembered, and need not derive from the heat of the controversy itself.

APPARATUS

G = London, Gray's Inn, MS 7, fols. 60r-61r
H = London, British Library, MS Cotton Cleopatra D.III, fols 7v-8r

VERA HISTORIA DE MORTE ARTHURI[1]

Igitur, finito prelii certamine [2](quod inter Arthurum regem Britonum et Modredum – non dico nepotem sed proditorem suum – committebatur), Modredo neci tradito, hinc inde pluribus prostratis multisque de inimicis relictis, rex etiam – etsi uictoriam adeptus – non tamen sine 5 cordis dampno abcessit. Vulnus etenim susceperat – licet non festinatam inferens mortem, tamen in proximo comminans futuram. Tandem pro adepta uictoria graciarum reddidit acciones omnium creatori sueque genetrici beatissime uirgini Marie; doloris acerbitatem pro strage 10 suorum habitam gaudio temperat triumphali. His ita peractis,[2] clipeo[3] innitens [4]post fatigacionem[4], refrigerandi gratia humi resedit; residens quatuor ex sue gentis primatibus accersiuit; accersitis iubet ut seipsum [5]diligenter armis[5] exonerent, ne forte incaucius agentes recentium[6] 15 uulnerum dolori cumulent dolorem. Rege quidem[7] exarmato, ecce quidam adolescens – pulcher aspectu,[8] statura procerus, [9]forma membrorum magnarum uirium preferens uirtutem[9] – carpebat iter, equi[10] tergo insidens, dextram uirga hulmea habens munitam. Que rigida erat, 20 non torta neque nodosa sed plana, et cuspide acuta ad modum lancee (sed quauis[11] lancea ad nocendum acutior) – siquidem preterito tempore artificis industria ad ignem rigida effecta (rigorque non dispari studio aquarum temperatus humore),[12] et uipereo infecta ueneno[13] ut quod forte 25 iaculata[14] minus noceret pro iaculantis defectu uirium uirus suppleret. Hic magnanimus adolescens per regem

1 hec est uera historia de morte Arthuri G: *no title in* H
2 ... 2 *omitted in* H
3 clipe G
4 ... 4 *omitted in* G
5 ... 5 armis diligenter H
6 recensium G
7 igitur H
8 aspectus G
9 ... 9 *omitted in* H
10 eq̄ (= eque?) G
11 plus H
12 ... 12 *omitted in* H
13 uēo G
14 iacula G

TRANSLATION

Accordingly, when the onslaught of the battle (which was being waged between Arthur king of the Britons and Modred — I dare not say his nephew but rather his betrayer) had ended, and Modred had been put to death, and here and there numerous warriors had been laid low and many of the enemy had been left for dead, the king — even though he had gained the victory — did not nevertheless withdraw without some misgiving in his heart. For he had sustained a wound — which, although it was not bringing an immediate death, nevertheless boded ill for the near future. At length by giving thanks he repaid the creator of all things and His mother the blessed Virgin Mary; he offset the bitterness of the remorse he had suffered for the loss of his men with his triumphal joy. When these things had been done, and, suffering from exhaustion, he was leaning on his shield, he sat down on the ground for the sake of recuperating; and while sitting there he summoned four of the leaders of his people; and when they have been summoned he orders them to disarm him carefully, lest perchance in proceeding carelessly they might increase the anguish of the pain of his wounds. When the king had been disarmed, suddenly a certain youth — handsome in appearance, tall in stature, evoking by the shape of his limbs a strength of immense power — took to the road, sitting on horse-back, with his right hand armed by a shaft of elm. This shaft was stiff, not twisted or knotted but straight, and sharpened to a point in the manner of a lance (yet sharper for inflicting injury than any lance) — since indeed in times gone by it had been fired to make it hard (and its hardness had been tempered with equal care by plunging it in water), and it had been daubed with adders' venom so that, what it might perhaps harm less when cast as a result of a deficiency in strength in the person casting it, it would make up for by spreading its poison. This audacious youth, proceeding

transiens [15]sed potius ante regem gradum sistens,[15] tale
iaculum iaculatur in regem et ipsius uulneribus grauibus
uulnus apposuit grauius. Quo facto, fugit concitus: sed non 30
effugit longius, quandoquidem rex, more impaciens, ut
miles strenuus hastam[16] uibrans in tergum[17] figit fugientis
et penetralia cordis transfixit. [18]Qui transfixus, spiritum
mox[18] exhalauit[19] uitalem. [20]Itaque, regis mortis auctore
morte excepto, summam ilico pallor regis oram[21] decolorat, 35
et diligencius intuentibus nunciabat eum non diucius aura
uitali fore fruiturum. Quo comperto, uultus illum arctius
amancium unda profluit lacrimarum et planctus affigit
uniuersos, quia eius simili Britannie desperant tueri liber-
tatem — siquidem, si iuxta uulgare prouerbium 'Raro bono 40
succedit melior', multo rarius optimo succedit optimus.[20]

Denique rex, parumper melioracioni[22] restitutus, iubet
se transuehi ad Venodociam, [23]quia in Auallonis insula
delectabili propter loci amenitatem perendinari proposuerat
(et quietis gracia[24] causaque uulnerum suorum mitigandi 45
dolorem).[23] Ad quam ubi peruentus est, medici pro sue
artis industria pro regis sunt solliciti uulneribus; sed rex
eorum sollicitudinibus[25] nullam salubrem persensit
efficaciam. Ob quod ipse de uite remedio desperatus,[26]
[27]Londoniensem ad se mandauit uenire archipresulem; qui 50
duorum episcoporum sibi adiunctorum contubernio —
scilicet Urien de Bangor et Urbegenii de Glamorgan — sui
copiam mandatus presentauit mandanti. (Sanctus quoque
Dauid Meneuensis archiepiscopus affuisset, nisi graui
corporis incommodio irretitus fuisset).[27] Hiis ergo presen- 55
tibus sue Christiane professionis confitetur excessus, seque
creatoris obsequio reddidit obnoxium. [28]Deinde sibi
famulantibus largitus regalis munificencie recompensat
famulatum; et Constantino filio ducis Cadoris Britannie
subiecit imperium.[28] Hiis itaque peractis, more ecclesiastico 60

---

15 ... 15 *omitted in* H

16 hasta G

17 terga G, *perhaps rightly (the author may have been thinking of phrases such as* terga dare, *etc.)*

18 ... 18 et mox spiritum H

19 ochalaum G

20 ... 20 *omitted in* H

21 *my correction*: hora G

22 melioracionem G

23 ... 23 *omitted in* H

24 *my conjecture*: gracie G

25 sollicitudis GH

26 deperatus G

27 ... 27 episcopos insule tocius ad se mandauit uenire H

28 ... 28 *omitted in* H

straight at the king but instead staying his course immediately in front of him, hurls the aforementioned missile into the king and so added a more serious wound to his already serious wounds. Having done this, he flees quickly: but does not escape for long, inasmuch as the king, brooking no delay, like an active soldier fixes the quivering spear in the back of the fleeing youth and pierces his innermost heart. Thus transfixed, the youth immediately breathed out his last breath. Accordingly, when the author of the king's death had himself been given over to death, a pallor immediately stains the king's last hour, and he explains to those people carefully watching over him that he is not to enjoy the breath of life for much longer. When this was disclosed, a wash of tears flowed down the faces of those who loved him dearly and lamentation overcame everyone, because they despaired that anyone could safeguard Britain's liberty like him — since, in fact, if according to the common proverb, 'a better man rarely succeeds a good man', much more rarely does an even better man succeed the one who is best.

At length the king, slightly restored by an improvement in his condition, gives orders to be taken to Gwynedd, since he had decided to sojourn in the delightful Isle of Avallon because of the beauty of the place (and for the sake of peace as well as for easing the pain of his wounds). When he had arrived there, physicians concerned themselves with the king's wounds with all the diligence of their art; but the king experienced no restorative remedy from their efforts. Because of this he despaired of any cure in this life, and he commanded the archbishop of London to come to him. The archbishop, in the company of two bishops allied to him — namely Urien of Bangor and Urbegen of Glamorgan — presented the fulfilment of the mandate to him who had directed it. (St David, the archbishop of Menevia [St David's] would also have been present if he had not been prevented by a serious bodily disease). With these prelates present, therefore, the king confesses his deviations from his Christian faith, and rendered himself answerable to his Creator's complaisance. Then he rewards his followers for their service with the generosity of royal munificence; and he settled the rule of Britain on Constantine son of Duke Cador. When these things had been

(diuina consecutus sacramenta) seculo nequam ualefecit extremum. [29] Et (sicud refert historia) extentus super silicium adinstar uere penitencium, tensis palmis ad celum in manus redemptoris suum commendabat spiritum. O quam dies ista lugubris! — quam digna[30] luctu, quam 65 planctu plena! — nec aliquando Britannie incolis absque doloris gemitu memoranda! Nec immerito: in ista enim die in Britannia iusticie tepuit disciplina, legum raruit obseruancia, pacis turbata est tranquillitas, libertatis est captiuata nobilitas; quia, cum Arturus gloriosus tollitur e 70 medio, Britannia singulari uictorie spoliata est priuilegio — quoniamquidem que dominabatur, penitus ancillatur. At ne longius a serie propositi uidear euagari, ad exequias defuncti noster calamus est reflectendus.[29]

Igitur prefati tres[31] episcopi [32] spiritum reuertentem ad 75 ipsum qui dedit illum summa oratione cum precum et deuocione condiunt[33] fragrancia,[32] ceteri regium corpus componunt regio more: balsamo et mirra condiunt et preparant sepulture commendandum. Die autem[34] sequenti corpus regis infuncti ad quandam paruam deferunt ecclesi- 80 am in honore sancte Dei genitricis [35] semper uirginis[35] Marie dedicatam, [36] sicut ipse uiuens deuouerat (ne alia suam terram susciperet terra).[36] [37] Ibi enim uolebat telluri recludi; ibi cupiebat carnem in suam originem redigi; ibi se mortuum eius commendabat tutele quam summa uenera- 85 batur deuocione.[37] Sed postquam ad prefate capelle peruentum est hostium, breuis et angustus aditus ingentis corporis glebe prohibebat ingressum, ob quod foris iuxta parietem, feretro superpositus,[38] sortitus est mansionem — cogente causa necessitatis: [39] nam sepiusdicte[40] capelle 90 aditus[41] ita fuit breuis et angustus ut in eam nullus intraret nisi latere premisso uno summo conamine[42] uirium et ingenio subintroduceret alterum.

29 . . . 29 *omitted in* H
30 dingna G
31 *omitted in* H
32 . . . 32 *omitted in* H
33 *?Read*: cum precum et deuocionum commendunt [*scil.* spiritum] fragrancia
34 *omitted in* H
35 . . . 35 *omitted in* H

36 . . . 36 sicut uiuens ipse deuouerat H
37 . . . 37 *omitted in* H
38 subpositus H
39 . . . 39 *omitted in* H
40 *?Read*: supradicte
41 *my conjecture*: auditus G
42 conamine *conjectured by* R. W. Hunt (see above, p.17 n. 4)

done, in the manner of the Church (following divine sacra-
ments) he bid his last farewell to this wicked world. And (as
the story relates), extended full-length on his hair-shirt in the
manner of those doing real penance, with his hands stretched
towards heaven he commended his spirit into the hands of his
Redeemer. O how sad was this day, how worthy of mourning,
how charged with lamentation, nor ever to be remembered
by inhabitants of Britain without cries of distress! Not un-
deservedly: for on this day the rigour of justice grew slack,
observance of the laws became a rarity, the calmness of peace
was shattered, the excellence of liberty was taken captive;
because, when glorious Arthur was taken from her midst,
Britain was deprived of its unique claim to victory — insofar
as she who held dominion is now totally enslaved. But lest I
seem to wander too far from the sequence of my narrative,
my pen ought to be turned back to the funeral rites of the
deceased king.

Therefore, the three aforementioned bishops commend the
soul returning to Him Who bestowed it with deepest prayer
through the sweetness of orisons and devotions; the others
lay out the royal corpse in a royal manner: they embalm it
with balsam and myrrh and prepare it to be committed to
burial. On the following day they take the corpse of the dead
king to a certain small chapel dedicated to the honour of the
Holy Mother of God, the perpetual Virgin Mary — just as the
king himself had appointed (so that no other earth would
receive his earthly remains). For in that place he wished to be
enclosed in the earth; there he wished his flesh to return to
its origin, there he commended his dead self to the vigilance
of Her whom he venerated with the deepest devotion. But
after the cortege arrived at the door of the aforementioned
chapel, the small and narrow opening prevented the entry of
the corpse's bulk; for that reason it was fated to a resting-
place outside adjacent to the wall, placed on its bier — the
force of necessity deciding this: for the entrance of the oft-
mentioned chapel was so small and narrow that no one could
enter it unless, having wedged one shoulder in, he drew in the
other with a great effort of strength and ingenuity.

Huius capelle incola fuit quidam heremita, qui, quanto fuerat auctionum[43] sordibus alienus, tanto gustauit 95 quiem[44] suauissime domus. Quam[45] maiores[46] intrant episcopi; pro regis anima diuina misteria celebrantur; et foris, ut doctum est, manet corpus defuncti.[39] Interim, episcopis exequias celebrantibus, aer tonat, terra nutat,[47] desuper crebro irruunt tempestates, fulgura choruscant, 100 aureque diuerse uariis se alternant uicibus. Demum, interposita breuissimi temporis morula, aeris subsecuta est caligo que fulgurum absorta est claritatem et tanta cecitate regii corporis obuoluit custodes, ut apertis oculis nihil uiderent. Hec[48] ab hora tertia usque ad nonam perdurat 105 assidue; [49] aer nullo tempore celebris horarum uicibus a tonitrui quiescit tumultu.[49] At deinde, cum caligo subducitur et serenitas restituitur, corporis regii nullas repperunt reliquias. Rex uero[50] raptus est ad paratam sibi mansionem; feretrumque[51] conspiciunt commendato frau- 110 datum. [52] De regis autem sublacione tedio afficiuntur, quousque inter eos magna uersatur ueri ambiguitas: 'unde ista uenerit potencia cuiusue raptus sit uiolencia?' − necnon adhuc presenti tempore tenebrae[53] cernuntur[54] ignorancie, ubi rex Arthurus locum[55] refrigerii sit sortitus.[52] Qua- 115 propter quidam dicunt quod uiuus est adhuc, et sanus et incolumis,[56] quia illis nescientibus raptus est. Quorum temerarie[57] opinioni nonnulli contradicunt, sine omni[58] dubietatis[59] scrupulo affirmantes illum mortis persoluisse debitum, tali innitentes argumento, quia, cum pretaxata[60] 120 fuit sublata caligo et claritas reuersa,[61] tumba seriata[62] apparuit presencium obtutibus et solide firmata et unita,

---

43 *my conjecture*: auctiorum G
44 *my conjecture*: quanto
corrected to quam G
45 qui (?) G
46 *my conjecture*: maior G
47 mutat H
48 hoc H
49 . . . 49 *omitted in* H
50 enim H
51 fereretrum G
52 . . . 52 *omitted in* H

53 *my conjecture*: tenebras G
54 *my conjecture*: cenantur G
55 *my conjecture*: locus G
56 incolumus G
57 temere H, *perhaps rightly*
58 *omitted in* H
59 dubietis H
60 pretacta H
61 *omitted in* G
62 serata H

The inhabitant of this chapel was a certain hermit, who, the more he had been remote from the squalor of the market-place, so much the more did he enjoy the serenity of this most peaceful dwelling. The senior bishops enter it; the holy services are performed for the soul of the king; and outside, as the story goes, the dead man's body remains. Meanwhile, while the bishops are performing the last rites, the air thunders, the earth quakes, storms pour down relentlessly from on high, lightning flashes, and the various winds blow in turns from their several quarters. Thereupon, after a short interval of the briefest space of time, a mist followed which absorbed the brightness of the lightning, and obscured the attendants of the royal corpse with such blindness that they saw nothing though their eyes were wide open. This mist continues uninterrupted from nine in the morning until three in the afternoon. At no point does the atmosphere, with the frequent passage of the hours, grow quiet from the crash of thunder. And finally, when the mist is dispersed and clear air restored, they find no trace of the royal corpse; for the king had been transported to an abode especially prepared for him; and they look on a bier deprived of that which had been committed to it. They are seized by annoyance as a result of the king's removal, to such an extent that great doubt concerning the truth arises among them: 'Whence will this mighty power have come? Through whose violence was he carried off?' – and even up to the present time shadows of ignorance are discerned, as to where King Arthur was destined to find his place of rest. Wherefore certain people say that he is still alive, both sound and well, since he was carried off without their knowledge. Others contradict their audacious conjecture, affirming without the slightest scruple of doubt that he paid the debt of death, relying on an argument of this sort, that, when the aforementioned mist had been dispersed and visibility had returned, the sealed tomb appeared to the gaze of those present to be both solidly closed and of one

ut pocius tota petra uideretur, integra et solida, [63]quasi
una cum altera cemento artificis et ingenio compacta.[63] In
cuius claustris regem [64]opinantur contineri,[64] cum eam 125
[65]ita compactam[65] inuenerunt et unitam. [66]Et quia talis
est facta inuencio,[67] inter eos non mediocris uersatur
dissensio.[68, 66]

Triginta et nouem annis in uirtutis[69] potencia, animi
sapiencia, discretionis prudencia, bellorum gloria imperium 130
Britannie gubernauit. Anno autem regni ipsius quadragesimo,
humane condicionis sortitus est terminum. [70]Igitur Arturo
defuncto, Constantinus Cadori ducis filius Britannicum
adeptus est regnum; et cetera.[70]

---

[63] . . . [63] et una quasi due H
[64] . . . [64] opina *followed by a*
lacuna G
[65] . . . [65] compactam ita H
[66] . . . [66] *here* H *interpolates an*
entirely different sentence: cuius
sepulchrum apud Glastoniam ubi
(ut dictum est) sepeliebatur tempore regis Ricardi cruce plumbea
super pectus, nomen eius inscrip-
tum declarante repertum est.
[67] inercio G
[68] discencio G
[69] uirtutum H
[70] . . . [70] H *offers an entirely*
different ending, as follows:
De quo uersus:
  Rex fuit Arthurus: rex est post
  regna futurus;

Prelia facturus uincet, numquam
  periturus.
Hic orbem rexit; sed Christus ad
  ethera uexit
Regem tam fortem, nec sensit
  corpore mortem.
Enoch translatum legimus super
  astra leuatum;
Ethereasque uias curru penetrauit
  Helias.
Isti pugnabunt, cum hostem non
  superabunt.
Sed magis Arthurus prudens ad
  prelia durus
Leuiathan feriet et ei uictoria
  fiet!

piece, such that it rather seemed to be one single stone, whole and solid, as if fashioned with the mortar and craft of a builder, one after the other. They think that the king is enclosed in its recesses, since they had discovered it already sealed and closed. And since this discovery had been made, there is no small disagreement among them.

He governed the realm of Britain for 39 years in the power of his strength, the wisdom of his mind, the acuteness of his judgement, and through his renown in battle. In the 40th year of his reign, he was destined to the end of the human lot. Therefore, with Arthur dead, Constantine, the son of Duke Cador, acceded to the British realm; and so on.

IV

MALORY: THE TRADITIONAL WRITER AND THE ARCHAIC MIND[1]

Derek Brewer

Malory is a traditional writer. That implies more than the basic fact that he was rehandling other people's writings. It implies a whole different ethos and attitude to his subject-matter and a quite different relationship between author, subject matter and 'world' than we who are conditioned by Neoclassical forms including the novel normally expect.[2] Many of the differences that arise between critics stem from the fundamental misunderstanding that derives from reading Malory as if he were writing within those criteria of literature that have developed since the seventeenth century. The modern models for Malory, if we must seek them, lie with folktale and with purely popular writing, both of which retain

1. The present paper was originally conceived in response to an invitation from the English Department of the University of Leiden to initiate a series of lectures in March 1981 with one on Sir Thomas Malory, to mark the publication of the translation of *Le Morte Darthur* into Dutch. I am grateful to the members of the Department in Leiden and also to those in the English Department of the University of Groningen where another version of the lecture was also given, for friendly interest and generous hospitality. A further version of the lecture was later delivered in April 1981 in the Universities of Bucharest, Napoca-Cluj and Iasi, with the happy coincidence of a translation of *Le Morte Darthur* into Romanian. I am much indebted for valuable comment and generous hospitality from the English Departments in those universities.

2. For a brief sketch of the development of Neoclassical concepts and their effect on Malory see my 'Introduction' in *Aspects of Malory*, ed. T. Takamiya and Derek Brewer, Cambridge, 1981, 1-8. For further detail see *Chaucer: The Critical Heritage*, ed. Derek Brewer, London, 1978, I, 3-24.

strong traditional elements. Alternatively, we must re-imagine for ourselves the qualities of medieval literature, either as popular and vernacular, or as governed by rhetorical learning and practice; for even a learned rhetorician in the Middle Ages was closer in his ideas about style to folktale than is a modern writer and above all a modern critic. It is for this reason that nowadays the 'naive' reader may come closer to Malory than the sophisticated one. I do not mean that Malory lacks art, but that he lacks sophisticated, ironic, i.e. modern, art. Thus men of action have tended to enjoy Malory while, until very recently, literary critics have despised him. My purpose in this essay is first of all to emphasize the traditional nature of Malory's writing; then to show that this is a clear evocation of what it has become common amongst anthropologists to call 'the savage mind' but which I shall call 'the archaic mind'; and then to show how Malory's consciousness of modernity is crucial to his sense of tragedy. Malory turns out to be, like most of us, both archaic and modern at the same time, but the clash between the two is particularly poignant with him.

A traditional writer receives a given story and is likely, as was certainly the case with Malory, to know this story in a number of different forms. The general story of Arthur, the relationship between Lancelot and Guinevere, the adventures of his knights of the Round Table, had been told many times and were surely common knowledge. In the West we are all in this situation still today, even in a culture so different. The consequence of knowing a story in various forms is that the body of material exists in what we may call a pre-verbal form, independent of any particular verbal realisation. A given story-teller, whether purely oral or using writing, may indeed translate or copy a particular text, but that particular text will not be the only source of his sense of the story. One result of this is that a big traditional story like the Arthurian story, though vague and general with many particular variations, acquires in the mind of all writers a sort of historical status. It is as it were a set of 'facts' coming from the past. Nowadays, since the seventeenth century, we have a much more clearly differentiated concept of history and fiction, but much of our historical knowledge is really of this same generic traditional kind. We all know that the First World War took place. We all have a few bits of information and a whole cloudy mist of feelings and ideas about it. The specific accuracy of any single fact beyond the most elementary is something few of us could guarantee. Our knowledge of it exists in a vague colourful area between history and fiction. Such areas were much more extensive in the Middle Ages when the distinction between history and fiction was both less established and somewhat differently conceived, and when also, for various reasons, the story of Arthur himself had come to be accepted as part of the true history of the British Isles. The story had been told so often with so many variations and additions that it was quite easy to treat it from different points of view. Many French authors of romances, for example, took quite different views of Arthur. Different writers could present roughly the same material in quite different ways, just as modern historians and modern critics present the same body of material or even the same text in different interpretations. Were we all medieval men we would not be writing critical accounts of the Arthurian legend: we would simply be rewriting our own version of that legend showing that Arthur was good or bad according to our lights.

Variability of interpretation was brought out many years ago by Professor Vinaver when he referred to the difference in medieval writing between *sens* and *matière*.[3] Repetition with variation is characteristic not only of medieval rhetoric, but also of all traditional writing. We may sum it up more generally by saying that 'the message dominates the matter'. The importance of this is that the traditional writer, having surveyed his material, then comes to some conclusion about its general drift, and may well in certain respects differ from his immediate predecessor or from other predecessors whom he knows, in evaluating the subject – again like a modern literary critic or historian. The traditional writer, when he has come to a conclusion about the truth of the 'inner message', feels no difficulty in altering, adapting or even in a relatively marginal way, inventing material which supports his view of

3. Vinaver's comment is in the introduction to his edition of Malory, *The Works of Sir Thomas Malory*, first edition 1947, now 2nd, revised ed., 3 vols. Oxford 1973, Vol.I, lxxiv et seq. All quotations from Malory are taken from this edition of the *Works*, numbered sequentially through three volumes, which are not henceforth noted.

the matter as opposed to the view of others.

The result is that the material and the story may be re-handled subject to the overriding condition that it remains the same story. This kind of rehandled narrative has been called 'plasmatic' and is characteristic of romance in general.

There has been much work over the last twenty or thirty years, follwing the first appearance of Professor Vinaver's great edition, in comparing Malory's work in detail with his actual or supposed sources, and we can now see how he constantly rehandled his sources to bring out certain aspects of the story and to suppress others. In doing this Malory follows the so-called 'rules' of folktale, or, as it would be preferable to say, of traditional literature. Very briefly summarized, these rules, which I have developed from Olrik,[4] show that a traditional story is by definition one that is re-told. It has an essential nucleus which makes it that story and no other story. It obeys as far as possible an internal logic of the story itself which may not − indeed often does not − directly reflect ordinary external everyday plausible sequences of cause-and-effect. The telling of the story involves rationalisation, that is to say, making the internal logic stronger either by eliminating those aspects which seem to conflict with the logic of the story as the writer conceives it, or by inventing other matter which may include motivations, descriptions, even episodes which seem to strengthen that internal logic. Writing of the traditional kind allows variation of emphasis so as to make the story more comprehensible and interesting. In particular episodes of *Le Morte Darthur* we see at work what Olrik calls the 'law of the single strand', whereby a single line of narrative is followed; the law 'of two characters only at a time' taking part in a scene; the 'law of three', by which things happen in threes (most notably with Lancelot's rescues of Guinevere), and so forth. It is vital to understand this general traditional style, so different from that of the novel, if we are to appreciate and understand Malory. Within his general traditionalism we will notice certain specific characteristics. One of the most important is that Malory

4. A. Olrick, 'Epic Laws of Folk Narrative' in *The Study of Folklore*, ed. A. Dundes, Englewood Cliffs, N.J., 1965, 129-41. See also Derek Brewer, 'The Gospels and the Laws of Folktale', *Folklore* 90 (1979), 37-51.

clearly set out to summarize not expand his story. One gets the impression, particularly in the early books, that Malory is setting out as much as anything quite literally to write a summary, as Caxton remarked. Even in the latter part of *Le Morte Darthur*, after the Grail story, where Malory invents a great deal of dialogue as part of his supreme artistic achievement, there is much cutting out of individual details and items from his sources so that he may concentrate on the single main strand of action, which only then does he illuminate, or as one may say, 'rationalise', by the invention of magnificent dialogue.

One aspect of this summarising compression is that Malory cuts out an enormous amount of physical realism from his sources with only a few exceptions that I will deal with later. The general habit of traditional writers, as we may see even in the Gospel writers, is to add physical realism in the progress of the story as part of the rationalisation, aiming to make the story more vivid, more impressive. Malory rarely, if ever, does this. His style is less concrete than that of his sources. Another aspect of his compression is the omission of much explanation. This has an effect similar to the omission of much physical realism. It gives the stories more autonomy, and juxtaposes a number of incidents that are themselves striking but not obviously connected. Such apparently arbitrary juxtaposition is particularly evident in the story of Balin[5] and less noticeable in the latter part of *Le Morte Darthur* but it always contributes something to Malory's work. Its success depends upon Malory's ability to select essential items in the story so that their juxtaposition in itself makes an effective pattern, without the need for sequences of plausible material cause-and-effect which his sources, the French romances, often supply to excess.

There is a paradox here. In one sense the omission of physical realism and of explanatory comment or sequences is non-traditional. That is, the normal development in traditional writing is for the story to be expanded by the various forms of rationalisation caused by the addition of realistic detail, by explanation through motivation imputed to the characters, or by the insertion of earlier incidents which

5. See especially Jill Mann, 'Taking the Adventure' in *Aspects of Malory* etc. Takamiya and Brewer as above, 71-92.

account for later incidents already present. Vinaver gives many examples of how the thirteenth-century French prose writers expanded the original tales by devices of this kind. These devices are not limited to thirteenth-century French prose writers. The Gospels themselves show the same factors at work, especially in the Gospel of St John. We find them again in the lives of Christ written during the Middle Ages, particularly in that attributed once to Bonaventura. Malory's summarising, therefore, though it can be parallelled occasionally by some scribes contemporary with him, and is traditional in so far as it asserts the traditional writer's freedom to change the presentation of his matter in accordance with his own purposes, nevertheless reverses the more usual traditional tendencies. The paradox is more extensive because by this apparently anti-traditional device, Malory tends to go back to his origins, becomes, in a sense, more primitive. He leaves untied all sorts of loose ends — again the story of Balin is an outstanding example — which a later writer would either eliminate or, more likely, tie up. In the early parts of the story of Balin Malory appears to be at an earlier stage of his development as a writer than say, after the Grail story, because he has not fully mastered that skill in retaining only essential elements which is part of the general art of omission on which so much of the greatness of his work depends. In general in the first section of *Le Morte Darthur* we find occasional muddle, even at the syntactical level, which shows Malory struggling with an enormous mass of material and not always succeeding in dropping what is necessary. The beautiful clarity of the latter parts is missing. On the other hand, in the early parts, we have a good deal more 'enchantment' or 'magic' not only specifically in such a character as Merlin and in a number of events, but in strange juxtapositions that are effective at the moment though they are never explained. 'Enchantment' thus contributes powerfully to Malory's work, and to its representation of the nature of experience, especially, as I shall show, to the paradoxical degree in which its strength is seen to have been superseded, or lost.

I turn to Malory's style. It is not surprising that this too can be characterised as a traditional style. A traditional style is in a somewhat different relationship to the world of experience than we have become accustomed to, at least in terms of Neoclassical commonsense since the seventeenth century. From the seventeenth century until very recently it has been felt that words should be the labels of things. An ideal style, we have been told, is 'concrete', the ideas rationally connected by cause-and-effect. The sequence is logical, follows an appropriate time sequence, and avoids repetition, hyperbole, punning or other 'rhetorical' elements which remove language from its capacity to give a close and careful report of the appearances of the world. This, to sum up, is an ideal of 'literalism', and being peculiarly objective is necessarily compensated for by a particular kind of subject-ivism. We must allow language to report inner feelings, as with the 'stream-of-consciousness technique', because feelings cannot be denied, for all their imprecision, but even such expressive language in modern times tends to be descriptive. We now tend normally to disregard or despise those aspects of language which are represented by commands, by direct expression of feeling, by appeals to emotion, or by sheer word-play, such as puns. By contrast, puns and other word-play are part of traditional language, as is hyperbole and repetition. Traditional style is also naturally and unself-consciously 'sententious', using proverbs and the received common wisdom in common expressions quite seriously. It is without irony. The 'literalism' which we now assume as an educational or intellectual ideal is a post-seventeenth-century phenomenon which is not shared by Shakespeare, or the language of the Book of Common Prayer, or by ordinary tellers of folktale, or by most medieval writers. On the whole, medieval people thought that literalism was comical. It is not surprising then that we find in Malory's style, as Mr Field, Professor Lambert and Professor Benson have clearly shown, repetition, hyperbole, sententiousness.[6] In particular, tra-ditional style attributes objective values to the world, independent of human judgment, in a way quite different from our modern feelings and concepts. The sharp distinction that we make between subjective and objective in ordinary 'common sense' terms is not made by a traditional writer.

6. P. J. C. Field, *Romance and Chronicle*, London, 1971; Mark Lambert, *Malory: Style and Vision in* Le Morte Darthur, New Haven and London, 1975; Larry D. Benson, *Malory's Morte Darthur*, Cambridge, Mass. and London, 1976.

For a traditional writer, values are objective and inherent in what is written about. It is consequently impossible to separate what we think of as 'subjective' value from 'objective' physical reality. In consequence there is for a traditional writer a natural identity of what is normal with what is natural and good, which often surprises a modern mind, or which the modern mind unhesitatingly rejects. There is no space to demonstrate these matters in detail here, but Lambert deals with them, though not in these terms, in the early part of his admirable book, and I quote the general conclusion that he draws about Malory's style and that of his period.

> The continuity of dialogue style and narrative style in our romances is quite clear. Fifteenth-century dialogue is a medium suited to presenting a reality in which there are central, normative truths. Such devices of romance prose narration as superlatives, qualitative details and conventional details also build a world with standards, norms, fixed values; a world in which *notatio* deals with things as objectively real and considerably more important than those dealt with by *effictio*. The common etymon of most of the devices I have described is a vision of reality in which what is most real, most matters, is the relation of the individual character or incident to normative values and standards; the common function of most of these devices is to project that vision.
>
> This is the common function of most of these devices, but not all. What such 'objective' devices as bare catalogues, ragged edge and blueprint details contribute to the prose romances (or can contribute) is a narrator who both believes in and reveres the value-centered world portrayed by the other devices. And because he believes in it, and cares about it, we do also.
>
> (Mark Lambert, *Malory: Style and Vision in Le Morte Darthur*, 1975, 55)

In the narrative style more generally contemplated, which Malory as a traditional writer creates, there is general agreement that what he is interested in is action rather than description, a generality of effect and not a local specificity, but with a sharp concentration on essential elements. Since

101

he is a traditional writer he also tends to leave at the heart of his work an enigma which arises partly accidentally (by his efforts to compress and concentrate on the essentials of an action, rejecting analysis and commentary), and partly from the traditional writer's sense that the story exists independent of and exceeding his own personal knowledge of it.

I turn now to the attitudes implicit in the imaginative world which Malory's traditional style creates. I exclude here anything outside the work such as deductions about the way the actual human being, Sir Thomas Malory, whoever he may have been, might have thought in ordinary real life about what he was doing. Yet it is characteristic of *Le Morte Darthur* as we have it, that it is a work in which the actual writer's implicit and indeed explicit attitudes are significant in its presentation.

As guidelines and examples I quote some key passages in the work, all apparently added by Malory himself to his sources, and occurring both early and late in *Le Morte Darthur*. The first is the Pentecostal Oath.

> . . . than the kynge stablysshed all the knyghtes and gaff them rychesse and londys; and charged them never to do outerage nothir morthir, and allwayes to fle treson, and to gyff mercy unto hym that askith mercy, uppon payne of forfiture [of their] worship and lordship of kynge Arthure for evirmore; and allwayes to do ladyes, damesels, and jantilwomen and wydowes [socour:] strengthe hem in hir ryghtes, and never to enforce them, uppon payne of dethe. Also, that no man take no batalyes in a wrongefull quarell for no love ne for no worldis goodis. So unto thys were all knyghtis sworne of the Table Rounde, both olde and younge, and every yere so were the[y] sworne at the hyghe feste of Pentecoste. (*Works*, p.120)

This passage emphasises the moral earnestness which characterises Malory's concept of knighthood throughout his work, and the reverence in which he holds it.

The next passage I take from the story of Tristram, central to *Le Morte Darthur*.

> And so Trystrams lerned to be an harper passyng all other, that there was none suche called in no contrey. And so in harpynge and on instrumentys of musyke in

102

his youthe he applyed hym for to lerne. And aftir, as he growed in myght and strength, he laboured in huntynge and in hawkynge — never jantylman more that ever we herde rede of. And as the booke seyth, he began good mesures of blowynge of beestes of venery and beestes of chaace and all maner of vermaynes, and all the tearmys we have yet of hawkynge and huntynge. And therefore the booke of [venery, of hawkynge and huntynge is called the booke of] sir Trystrams.

Wherefore, as me semyth, all jantyllmen that beryth olde armys ought of ryght to honoure sir Tristrams for the goodly tearmys that jantylmen have and use and shall do unto the Day of Dome, that thereby in a maner all men of worshyp may discever a jantylman frome a yoman and a yoman frome a vylayne. For he that jantyll is woll drawe hym to jantyll tacchis and to folow the noble customys of jantylmen. 　　　　(*Works*, p.375)

This passage marks first of all the connectedness of various skills which characterise a gentleman. Since the capacity to learn such skills is inherited, another form of connectedness, with ancestors, is demonstrated. The unity of the class is set off against other inferior classes, and is morally noble by implication. The united aggregate of gentlemanlike characteristics is timeless, for it extends from of old to the ultimate Day of Doom. I quote next the passage about the coming of May, much nearer the end.

And thus hit passed on frome Candylmas untyll [after] Ester, that the moneth of May was com, whan every lusty harte begynnyth to blossom and to burgyne. For, lyke as trees and erbys burgenyth and florysshyth in May, in lyke wyse every lusty harte that ys ony maner of lover spryngith, burgenyth, buddyth, and florysshyth in lusty dedis. For hit gyvyth unto all lovers corrayge, that lusty moneth of May, in somthynge to constrayne hym to som maner of thynge more in that moneth than in ony other monethe, for dyverce causys: for than all erbys and treys renewyth a man and woman, and in lyke wyse lovers callyth to their mynde olde jantylnes and olde servyse, and many kynde dedes that was forgotyn by neclygence.

For, lyke as wynter rasure dothe allway arace and

103

deface grene summer, so faryth hit by unstable love in man and woman, for in many persones there ys no stabylité: for [w]e may se all day, for a lytyll blaste of wyntres rasure, anone we shall deface and lay aparte trew love, for lytyll or nowght, that coste muche thynge. Thys ys now wysedome nother no stabylité, but hit ys fyeblenes of nature and grete disworshyp, whosomever usyth thys.

Therefore, lyke as May moneth flowryth and floryshyth in every mannes gardyne, so in lyke wyse lat every man of worshyp florysh hys herte in thys worlde: firste unto God, and nexte unto the joy of them that he promysed hys feythe unto; for there was never worshyp-full man nor worshypfull woman but they loved one bettir than another; and worshyp in armys may never be foyled. But firste reserve the honoure to God, and secundely thy quarell muste com of thy lady. And such love I calle vertuouse love.

But nowadayes men can nat love sevennyght but they muste have all their desyres. That love may nat endure by reson, for where they bethe sone accorded and hasty, heete sone keelyth. And ryght so faryth the love now-adayes, sone hote sone colde. Thys ys no stabylyté. But the olde love was nat so. For men and women coude love togydirs seven yerys, and no lycoures lustis was betwyxte them, and than was love trouthe and faythe-fulnes. And so in lyke wyse was used such love in kynge Arthurs dayes.

Wherefore I lykken love nowadayes unto sommer and wynter: for, lyke as the tone ys colde and the othir ys hote, so faryth love nowadayes. And therefore all ye that be lovers, 'calle unto youre remembraunce the monethe of May, lyke as ded quene Gwenyver, for whom I make here a lytyll mencion, that whyle she lyved she was a trew lover, and therefor she had a good ende.   (*Works*, pp.119-20)

Here we see the connection between human feelings and the passage of the seasons, especially between the revivifi-cation of spring and the recall of noble 'service' and deeds of good nature. We see also, imaged in the progress of the seasons, the danger of breaking the loyalty, the connected-ness, of true love, bringing about instability, uncertainty, fragmentation. Properly speaking a man's love should be loyally kept to God, to his friends, and to one particular woman, which will make him bold and virtuous. So it once was, but is not nowadays.

I reinforce this latter passage with Malory's remark, when Agravain and Mordred catch Lancelot and Guinevere together, that 'whether they were abed other at other maner of disportis, me lyste nat thereof make no mencion, for love that tyme was nat as love ys nowadayes' (*Works*, p.1165). Malory's probable source says that they were in fact in bed together.

My final quotation is the famous address to the English, very near the end.

> Lo ye all Englysshemen, se ye nat what a myschyff here was? For he that was the moste kynge and nobelyst knyght of the worlde, and moste loved the felyshyp of noble knyghtes, and by hym they all were upholdyn, and yet myght nat thes Englyshemen holde them contente with hym. Lo thus was the olde custom and usayges of thys londe, and men say that we of thys londe have nat yet loste that custom. Alas! thys ys a greate defaughte of us Englysshemen, for there may no thynge us please no terme.   (*Works*, pp.1229)

Here we see marked the tragic disloyalty and instability of the English.

These quotations, which could be added to very considerably especially on a smaller scale, give examples of Malory's characteristic values which it is most important to recognise and to get right. We note the moral earnestness expressed with traditional sententiousness which underlies all his interest in Arthurian adventure, well summed up by Lambert and expressed in that concept of knighthood which is the complex dominant value of his world. Knighthood comprises a stable social class with normative values which extend connectedly from harping to hunting, hawking and noble behaviour as appropriate to a gentleman. A part of a gentleman's behaviour is the practice of virtuous love, and love itself is to be connected with other aspects of a gentleman's life and nobility and also with the seasons of the world.

One may sum up Malory's general attitude as unitive of experience of the world; or conversely, as expressing the view

105

that the world itself is unitive, and that experience comprises a continuum between the observer and the external world, all of them sharing the same values. There is no break, no dividing line between world and book. Something of this is implied by Mr Field, and also by Professor Lambert when he emphasises the singleness of Malory's tone. It is also implied when Lambert says rightly, when developing the notion of an honour/shame culture in Malory, that Malory is himself part of that culture of honour and shame. He does not stand apart and observe it like a modern anthropologist; he expresses it unselfconsciously.

The essence of this unitive view of the world as found in *Le Morte Darthur* lies in seeing the world as itself intrinsically a network of personal relationships. Malory cuts out almost every other element. The touches that he leaves in of realistic description, of causal relationship and so forth and those few realistic touches that he adds are all in the cause of establishing personal relations. In this respect I would qualify Vinaver's remark that Malory, continued, though in a different way, the 'elucidations' of the thirteenth century French prose romancers. Malory does not elucidate, he *connects*. An interesting specific example amongst many occurs in a book of Tristram when Tristram goes to sleep with the wife of Segwarides (*Works*, p.394ff. Note on page 1460). Vinaver notes that Malory adds some realistic details to the French, as that they had a light supper, and that Tristram's wound bled on both the oversheet and the undersheet and the blood was discovered by candlelight. Of course this adds to the visual element in the scene but these details are not there for their visual vividness, nor are they an example, as Field suggests *à propos* similar added realistic details elsewhere, of Malory's imagination working in a more fervent active way. The details are primarily there to make clear the connections between husband, wife and lover. The light supper establishes the cheerful domesticity existing between Tristram and the lady (who incidentally is never named). The details of the bloody sheets illustrate both the relationship between Tristram and the lady and the relationship between the lady and her husband, because they make it so plain how it was that the husband detected his wife's infidelity. A further most interesting example of Malory's method, and of his tendency to repeat, is the similar but far more expert and

106

significant episode much later, when Lancelot's cut hand is found by Meleagaunt to have bloodied Queen Guinevere's bed (*Works*, pp.1131-2). The concrete realism is minimal, but every detail counts in making significant connections between individuals.

Another aspect of this unitive presentation of the world is the sense of the objective existence of moral values found, not only in Malory, but in many writers of his time, and in the way in which apparent description is itself primarily evaluative. Such evaluative references, which are always general, and tend to refer things as being 'the best of their kind', are common in romance generally and extend certainly as far as Spenser. Such evaluation tends to arouse the ire of the modern critic, who wishes to be assured, even if fictively, of the separate, visualisable, but morally neutral existence of physical objects. Spenser has been severely condemned for his failure to visualise and his tendency to describe only in morally evaluative terms. But Malory is much the same. Even when he attributes substantial personal expression to a character as, for example, in the complaint of the Fair Maid of Ascolat she is made to express a generalised emotion, in a sententious style, which is deeply moving. As both Field and Lambert point out, no speaker in Malory has an individualised style.

The absence of identifiably individualistic speech is connected with an almost complete absence of 'characterisation' (i.e. of specially identifying idiosyncratic traits of personality) which many critics have remarked upon. Such traits occasionally arise, as Gawain's taste for fruit in the episode of The Poisoned Apple (*Works*, p.1048), or his increase of strength up to midday, and consequent decline (*Works*, p.1216). The first of these traits seems to be peculiar to Malory, and it is significant that it contributes to the action, not to any overall impression of Gawain's personality. The second is found in the sources, but again contributes to the impression we gain of the episode as a whole, not to Gawain's personality. The contours of individuality as such are of little interest to Malory, as to most traditional writers. By contrast there is an absolutely passionate feeling for the cohesion of the group, most famously expressed in King Arthur's lament when he remarks that 'quenys I myght have inow, but such a felyship of good knyghtes shall never to togydyrs in no company'

(*Works*, p.1184). In their final speeches both Guinevere and Lancelot express sorrow for the tragic loss of the group rather than for their sinfulness or for any other specific reason. The absence of individualising characterisation is another aspect of the absence of any interior or psychological knowledge about the characters. We have a strong feeling for their existence, but most of our knowledge about their thoughts and feelings is very general and mainly based on deduction from what they say or do not say. Nor are they, except in rare moments of high climax, at all expressive.

The unity of the author with his world, and what Professor Lambert rightly emphasises as his 'reverence' for that world, deserves emphasis. Malory's world is conceived of as having objective validity, whatever the artistic manipulation involved in its effective presentation. And he was at one with that world, sharing its values unselfconsciously, believing in its historical existence, attributing to it supreme value as an episode in our history. It is not too extravagant to say that the world thus envisaged is 'sacred' for Malory, divinely ordained, requiring our reverence. There are several implications and one qualification of this. One implication which is very important, and which both Field and Lambert remark, is that in this world *there is no irony*. It is true that occasionally, within the story, characters will use irony or an ironical inflexion in talking to each other, usually by means of understatement, which is a very special kind of irony familiar in the English heroic tradition from the Anglo-Saxons. But the world itself is not presented ironically. Malory does not give us 'an ironic culture', (an expression to which I shall return). One consequence of this is that we must strongly resist the growing tendency to refer to 'the Narrator' instead of referring to the author or Malory. It is strange that under the force of modern fashion and of the modern world-view, both Lambert and Field, who have done so much to establish the unitive character of Malory with his world, still occasionally do their best to refer to the Narrator, as if he were an ironic narrative *persona* whose views might well be quite different from those that the work itself is ultimately designed to convey. That cannot be. There is no Narrator, there is only the author, who tells us that his name is Sir Thomas Malory. It is, however, here that we do begin to come to an important qualification. Malory has a special sense not only of the past, which is general among traditional writers, but of 'the past-ness of the past', which is something different. Malory refers, for example, to virtuous love as being in the past; nowadays such love is not to be found. To this extent he distances his own imaginative world from the world that he actually lives in. There is here the beginning of a crack or division between the author and the world he describes which is near to what we ourselves are always conscious of in fiction. It is a small crack, but it makes way for something more important still, which is revealed in the address to Englishmen. Malory there recognises, as he relives the experience of his chosen world in the past, that *even in the past* that world also contained treacherous Englishmen. For Malory the unitive world that he values is held together by loyalty which is love. Part of love is sexual, but really that is relatively a small and indeed rather awkward part. Loyalty, that great traditional virtue of medieval thought and feeling, creates the stability which Malory so much cherishes. Yet he sees that even in that Arthurian world, which he so vividly recreates, where personal loyalties link all together in a stable society which is the absolute paradigm of the Popperian Closed Society — even there, we find that disloyalty has penetrated and dissolved the most precious bonds. This disloyalty, this fluidity, in a would-be stable world, is the significant element in the tragedy he perceives.

To summarise the argument so far, Malory is a traditional writer who exemplifies with particular clarity the traditional unitive view which conceives of the world as inherently con-nected on the basis of personal relationships extending to the physical world. This connected world has inherent objective moral value, and is 'sacred'. It is in principle comprehensible, though the golden arbitrary thread of enchantment pierces it in parts. The world is rooted in the past, but conceives of no desirable change and is essentially timeless. It is described in the traditional style which reflects the unity between author and world, sees actions and people in terms of good and evil, rather than of individual personality, and invokes the inherited wisdom of the community. This summary is not a complete account of the implicit attitudes and fundamental structures of the *book* itself, *Le Morte Darthur*. If it were, there would be no tragedy; but it is fundamental to the book and needs to be categorised further. The world of *Le Morte*

Darthur is the product of what I propose to call 'the archaic mind', and I must now momentarily digress to describe what is meant by that term. Once established it will clarify certain of Malory's most marked characteristics and allow us to understand more fully the paradoxical nature of his great literary achievement.

The concept of 'the archaic mind' goes back to what the anthropologists call 'the savage mind'. This notion is deep in nineteenth century and perhaps even eighteenth century thought but has been invoked with some considerable frequency in the last twenty years. In the early twentieth century it was assumed that the savage mind was something quite different from the modern mind, being pre-logical and merely associative. Yet from this notion of the savage mind it is likely that T. S. Eliot drew his famous concept of 'the dissociation of sensibility' which he located rather vaguely in the seventeenth century.[7] In Eliot's view, before the seventeenth century the English mind perceived a connected unity of experience, but after the seventeenth century thought and feeling became disjunct, and from this separation arose many modern ills. Eliot's formulation has been both used and attacked considerably and I do not suppose that nowadays anybody would like to claim any kind of sharp break between an earlier and a later world taking place in the seventeenth century. There are some indeed who maintain that the idea is totally false and reflects only nostalgia for a golden age. That however is in its turn too simple a view. Recent anthropologists, philosophers and historians of science have made it plain that a really major cultural change did take place in Western European history whose centre can be located in the seventeenth century and from which modern science and essentially the modern world-view, so different from the traditional, arise.[8] For a relatively recent account of this by a philosopher without literary interests I refer to Professor Ernest Gellner's *Legitimation of Belief*.[9] Gellner

7. T. S. Eliot, 'The Poetry of Donne' in *Selected Essays 1917-32*, 1932.

8. J. F. Kermode delivers a strong attack in *Romantic Image*, London, 1961. For a general discussion of the problem, with bibliography, see Jack Goody, *The Domestication of the Savage Mind*, Cambridge, 1977.

9. E. Gellner, *Legitimation of Belief*, Cambridge, 1974.

110

accepts, for the purposes of argument, a polarity between the savage or primitive mind, and the modern or scientific mind, using anthropological work to support his argument. For our purposes it is sufficient to accept the polarity for the convenience of the description while remembering first, that there are intermediate stages between the two extremes, and second, what is even more important, and only implicit in most discussion, that *every mind*, at *every* period, in *every* culture, retains within itself aspects both of the so-called savage mind and of the modern or scientific mind. It is partly for this reason that it is desirable to avoid the connotations of the words 'savage' or 'primitive'. They still have an aura of nineteenth-century superiority and sense of difference which I wish to avoid. At the same time it is true that the savage mind, so-called, dominates earlier cultures, and it is certainly the case that the modern, or scientific mind is extremely unusual, and has only developed since the seventeenth century, even if its traces can be found as far back as our knowledge of any kind of human mind at all. So it is convenient and less patronising to refer to the 'archaic' mind and to contrast it with the 'modern' or 'scientific' mind. We avoid too sharp a break between the two in the history of culture by insisting that every mind is composed of elements of both archaic and modern, while recognising that most earlier cultures are predominantly archaic, and that our effective cognitive modern processes are scientific in a way that is culturally unusual. In Gellner's terminology the archaic mind is the mind which is 'enchanted' or which accepts 'magic'; in other words, sees the world as comprehensible, meaningful, morally significant, even if locally baffling. It is both objectively real and inclusive of ourselves. To quote Gellner, what he calls the savage mind, and I call the archaic mind, is 'characterised by a failure to separate cognitive functions from others, by the fusion of nature and culture, of knowledge and of social charter.' (p.180). The archaic mind generates 'a world which is "meaningful", cosy and "human" rather than cold, mechanical and unhuman.' In other words, it generates a unitive world connected in terms of personal relationships.

Gellner insists on the connectedness of the archaic mind, and its refusal to separate cognitive functions from others. The connectedness is between observation, thought, feeling, and values. He also points to the archaic mind as being

111

incapable of distinguishing between the world of nature and the world of culture, just as Malory in his muddled way says that love is mixed up with leaves and the burgeoning of flowers. The archaic mind, just like Malory's, sees the world in strongly moral and human terms also with many irregularities. That is, the archaic mind is idiosyncratic, and yet considers its idiosyncratic patterns to be normative. One may see a particularly good example of normative yet idiosyncratic pattern in the notions of honour and shame that characterise not only Malory's world, but the whole of the archaic world of European civilisation. Enchanted, idiosyncractic, normative, all these add up to that unitive or, as some philosophers prefer to call it, monistic or holistic, world and experience of the world, which critics have seen so strongly exemplified by Malory.

Gellner contrasts with the archaic world our modern world of 'regular morally neutral, magically un-manipulable fact' (p.180). Gellner continues: 'Far from representing some kind of normality, a natural starting point, historically it is a great oddity. It is separated from most or all other worlds in which men have lived by a profound chasm' (p.180).

Our world is thus in principle regular, whereas Malory's world is in principle irregular. Malory's world is far from being morally neutral. He limits his world to human beings and they are all conceived of in moral terms. It is a world in which fact can be manipulated by such wizards as Merlin as in the earlier part of *Le Morte Darthur*. Gellner remarks that 'enchantment works through idiosyncracy, uniqueness, spontaneity, a magic which is tied to the identity and individuality of the participants . . .' (p.189). We may doubt the clarity of the notions of identity and individuality in Malory in a literal sense, but it is unquestionably true that Malory's world is full of individuals, for it is they who constitute the group. Gellner by no means excludes the emergence of the re-creation in modern times of attitudes to the world which I have called 'archaic', though he despises them. He refers contemptuously to 'the new anthropomorphism of our age, the illusion that the universe can best be understood, and human fulfillment best be pursued through the sloppiest, most "spontaneous", least disciplined thought . . .' (p.192). For him religion, art, culture, sport are mere frills and are equally archaic. But he also refers to the fact that in 'most of our life,

112

there is a complex symbiosis of diverse conceptual styles' (p.193). That is, we all maintain simultaneously a number of different, not necessarily compatible, attitudes to the world. We all include in our total mentality both the archaic and the modern. But Gellner in his contrast of the modern with the archaic mind goes on to insist that there is 'a very important general trait of modern societies: the emergence of what may be called ironic cultures' (p.193). 'They contain claims, assertions, which *sound* cognitive, and which in other non-ironic cultures would indeed have been such; but there, it is somehow understood that they are not fully serious, not commensurate nor continuous with real knowledge' (pp.193-4). For Gellner the only kind of real knowledge is scientific knowledge, though the archaic is 'more colourful, human, cosier' (p.194). Nowadays we can only, in so far as we are modern (and we are predominantly modern), believe in archaic culture in an 'ironic', or alternatively, a symbolic way. (This is indeed the only way by which a modern mind can entertain traditional religious 'truth', as symbol.)

To summarise, the archaic mind differentiates much less clearly than the scientific mind, is less specialised. Moral, psychological and material objects of perception are not clearly distinguished and disconnected from each other. Phenomena are conceived of as indivisible amalgams of personalised and material qualities. The archaic mind attends to all these qualities with reverence, and believes in them with total conviction. Deeply held convictions which are crucial to a general world view are spread widely throughout the structure of the archaic world. It follows that in an archaic world, where everything is connected with everything else, if one particular element crumbles much else will collapse with it. The archaic world has a much more widely diffused sense of what is vital or, as we may say, what is 'sacred', that is, of elements which demand our complete devotion. The archaic mind is under a deep obligation to sustain all its elements. It is not fragmented, specialised into many autonomous elements, as is the case with the modern mind.

It is for this reason that the concept of loyalty, which binds all together, is so crucial in the archaic mind, and consequently in most medieval culture. Particularly where the world is conceived of in highly personalised terms, as in Malory's case, where he concentrates so strongly on personal

113

relationships, loyalty must be all. If that bond breaks then indeed chaos is come again.

For us as modern people many of these archaic concepts are difficult to realise because we are, by definition, whether we like it or not, predominantly relativistic, pluralistic. We have an essentially symbolic or, as Gellner would say, an ironic view of the universe, whereas for the archaic mind contact with the universe is direct and 'real'. Moreover, we have been taught to regard many traditional values as irrelevant to our modern situation. The most obvious example is chastity. All previous periods, until very recently, of Western culture considered chastity a sacred virtue. The developments of modern technology have removed the utilitarian base and with it the barrier against all the manifold forces that necessarily operate against chastity. To many people nowadays the concept of chastity and particularly the supreme value set upon it by earlier western European Christian culture is totally incomprehensible. Yet if we want to understand earlier periods of our own culture, including Malory's work, we have to imagine our way back into it.

Another clear example is the concept of bravery or courage. It seems almost impossible to convey to today's young in the West any conscious sense that there is a glory in war. They are, of course, equally as or even more personally aggressive in all sorts of ways than their forebears, but the modern situation, intellectual, technological and social, has apparently removed almost all the glory from fighting. This itself can be noted in literary terms as following the slaughter of the First World War and registered in a remarkable passage in Hemingway's *A Farewell to Arms* (1929):

> I did not say anything. I was always embarrassed by the words sacred, glorious and sacrifice and the expression in vain. We had heard them, sometimes standing in the rain almost out of earshot, so that only the shouted words came through, and had read them, on proclamations that were slapped up by bill-posters over other proclamations, now for a long time, and I had seen nothing sacred, and the things that were glorious had no glory and the sacrifices were like the stockyards at Chicago if nothing was done with the meat except to bury it. There were many words that you could not stand to hear and finally only the names of places had

114

dignity. Certain numbers were the same way and certain dates and these with the names of the places were all you could say and have them mean anything. Abstract words such as glory, honour, courage, or hallow were obscene beside the concrete names of villages, the numbers of roads, the names of rivers, the numbers of regiments and the dates. (p.195)

It is worth placing this remarkable quotation against Malory. The Hemingway passage is of course far more rhetorical and archaic than it pretends to be, and deserves analysis for its own sake. But here it will be enough to register its message as exactly expressive of what the modern mind rejects as archaic. Just think what Lancelot would make of it. The sacredness of war cannot be understood by the modern mind, nor can patriotism, nor the sacred obligations of honour, nor chastity, nor the hierarchical structure of society. We need to recreate these archaic concepts in our minds as we read Malory, and such is his power of imagination and style, such is the rooted-ness of our basic feelings about life in the archaic, that Malory succeeds.

Yet his success is the greater because he does more than express and for us recreate the archaic world. Malory presents us with a tragedy which is the break-up of that world. In order to consider that tragic conclusion, we may recall the small but sinister cracks that I mentioned earlier, and then pay particular attention to a most significant and interesting figure in Malory's story of Tristram; the figure of Dinadan, the only knight who does not take knighthood seriously. Vinaver says of him:

Dinadan is perhaps the most human, if not the most attractive character in the French Romance, and there is nothing more sobering in Arthurian literature than the gentle irony of this companion of Tristram *qui cherche le sens du monde, mais point n'en peut trouver*. He seems to have dropped almost by accident into the mad kingdom of Arthur where people never greet each other except with the point of a spear and never seem to look for anything they have a reasonable chance of finding. He is at a loss to understand why everybody should long for the unattainable favours of haughty ladies when real human love is such a simple and enjoyable thing, when

115

it can make anyone *gai, riant et envoisié* as long as one does not ask too much of it. Nor can he grasp the significance of the rigid customs governing the life of a knight-errant and constantly forcing him to face danger; if only cowards are allowed to live happily Dinadan is prepared to be a coward, and if the observance of knightly customs means falling from one's horse and suffering other similar hardships he would much rather give up chivalry once and for all. And it exasperates him to find that other knights are incapable of understanding this simple remark of his: *ma couardise me fet vivre, et vostre hardement vos fet orendroit estre a pié*.

It is instructive to see how many such passages Malory deleted, and how much he shortened those which he could not delete. But it is perhaps no less significant that much as he resented Dinadan's criticisms of chivalry he was unable to make them innocuous. Dinadan is still very much the same in Malory as he is in the French; he has fewer opportunities of 'scoffing', but he says enough to question the wisdom of chivalry as an institution. All that Malory really succeeds in doing is to reveal from time to time his own attitude to such things and the inevitable conflict between himself and his French book.   (*Works*, pp.1147-8)

Dinadan, with his irony, his cowardice, his refusal of faithful love, his lack of reverence, in a word his utilitarian willingness to collaborate with anyone stronger than himself, is genuinely modern. He expresses what any modernistic critic feels when confronted with Malory's world and attitudes.

There are, however, other things besides Dinadan in his own vision of Arthurian chivalry which Malory does not like but which he cannot avoid. He has to recognise, as he works through his narrative, with his capacity for facing the essential truth of experience, the presence in his archaic world, not only of the emblematic figure of Dinadan, but of other elements which inevitably lead to its destruction.

He sees that we Englishmen are always unfaithful, not only now but in the past. In the case of Malory's art the English stand for everybody, for the human race as a whole. We almost all betray ourselves and each other when we are put under sufficient stress, as much literature and, alas, most of our experience, tell us.

In terms of the destruction of his own world, Malory sees betrayal, and he sees some elements of it even in the best of men, in Lancelot himself. He sees how the company of comrades, the connectedness of a unitive universe, may be broken up simply by the normal activities, even the purely accidental activities, of those who comprise it. The death of Gareth has been singled out by critics as the breaking point *par excellence* of Malory's world. Gareth with his devotion to Lancelot, and the honourable love and good will between them, exemplify the best of the loyalty of the archaic world, yet Lancelot inadvertently kills Gareth, who is himself un-armed in order that he shall not be found fighting Lancelot. This comes in the sequence of those significant three rescues of the Queen by Lancelot which are themselves a larger part of the process of mixed intention and accident which brings about the destruction of the knighthood. Many other episodes in *Le Morte Darthur* may be called to mind which illustrate the difficulty of maintaining the bonds, not only of love and loyalty, but of personal interconnectiveness, which must hold the archaic world together.

There are more radical elements to be noted in the later books. It is no accident that in these there is practically no recourse to 'enchantment', 'magic'. They give far less sense of the arbitrary inexplicable chanciness yet exciting potentiality of an archaic world. Although Malory's latest part of the *Le Morte Darthur*, after the Grail story, does not progress purely in terms of causality, there is nevertheless in it a kind of con-nectedness different from that archaic, arbitrary association or mixture, that idiosyncratic patterning, which characterises the earlier parts. In the latest part there is a much stronger sense of physical cause-and-effect at work, and it is particu-larly notable that such causality is sometimes neutral, to use Gellner's description of the modern world. The best example is the adder in the heathbush which causes the knight to draw his sword and thus to precipitate the final disastrous battle between Mordred's army and Arthur's. This is an example of genuine causality. Had the sword not been drawn the nego-tiations would conceivably had led to peaceful resolution. But the sword was drawn, and as a direct result the watching armies thought that fighting had broken out, and battle was joined. The cause is absolutely trivial and morally neutral. In one sense it is accidental, in that, within the bounds of the story, something else might have happened, but in another sense it is part of a morally neutral, quite unfortunate but ineluctably linked series of causes and effects which produce the final tragedy. It need not have happened, but that is exactly what the situation must be for a modern tragedy, because the modern mind by definition conceives the world as being ultimately without value, without purpose and without direction.

In these last books time has become linear in the way that we recognise 'modern' time to be. One might multiply examples of the modernity of the situation in the series of stories towards the end of *Le Morte Darthur* which constitute a steady line of development which has much more feeling of historical causality as seen by the modern mind, than have the stories in the earlier parts.

The tragedy for Malory is indeed the advent of the modern world. The tragedy is the collapse of the archaic world. It is the fall of Arthur, with its echoes of the fall of Rome and more remotely of the fall of Adam himself. Even in that great founding myth of our culture, the story of the Fall of Man, both archaic and a modern co-exist, and it tells how time destroys the timeless. The Garden of Eden is itself a vision of the fully realised archaic world existing in a timeless period of myth when culture and nature are fused, where there is a sense of close communion between mankind and God, where the objective material world (including the forbidden fruit) is the sacred world of value and meaning. But it is of the nature of our experience that even in the Garden of Eden there is the serpent; the serpent of time, of covetousness, envy, individualism and consequently disloyalty. Moreover, it is this principle of evil which is connected with change, is connected with time. Even in the Garden of Eden are the seeds of the modern world.

The greatness of *Le Morte Darthur* in part lies in its presentation of the existence of causality, of tragedy, within the beloved archaic world, and the deeply moving way in which our human dilemma is represented in terms of the eternal recreation of the archaic and the irresistable movement from the archaic to the modern, from life to death.

And yet *Le Morte Darthur* does not arrive at the one-sided nihilism which characterises our own particular phase of modern literary culture, at the deep though inevitably self-contradictory despair and disgust of a Sartre or a Beckett. If it is true that the seeds of tragedy are already sown in the very nature of the garden of Eden, if disloyalty is necessarily implicit even in the highest reaches of the Arthurian ideal knighthood, it is also the case that only from that archaic world can any values at all originate. Values are the product of the archaic, not of the modern mind which has necessarily abjured them. Only in so far as values survive can we evaluate tragedy. If the world was not, and is not, at least partially good, partially therefore archaic, no loss or damage to the world can be tragic. A modern nihilistic view of existence cannot be a tragic view because there is by definition no standard whatsoever by which to judge it to be so. It simply is as it is.

In *Le Morte Darthur*, Arthurian knighthood is destroyed, but life is carried on, if in a colder, bleaker, more modern world. Malory's perception of this can be seen even in formal terms. Although Professor Vinaver was mistaken in seeing *Le Morte Darthur* in terms of eight entirely separate would-be novels, he was surely right in perceiving that Malory, though he was following earlier models, nevertheless was creating something of a modern form. It is of the essence of *Le Morte Darthur* that it confronts archaic material with modern constraints and even modern formal constrictions. The greatness of Malory is that he was to maintain the dichotomy in creative tension.

This also explains why Malory is sometimes erroneously described as nostalgic. He is not nostalgic in so far as that may be an enfeebling longing for what can never be again. But it is true that Malory perceives the originating values of a partially lost archaic world, and he is under no illusion about the real nastiness of the present world, whether of the fifteenth or, by implication, of the twentieth century. To see nostalgia in Malory is to mistake the nature of his entirely legitimate pain in contemplating what the world is actually like.

But on the other hand it would be equally mistaken to emphasise tragedy alone in Malory. We come back to the original point. Tragedy cannot exist independent of an originating world of values which we can hope in principle to understand and find meaningful, which includes the brotherhood of man, the unity of man and nature, the values of courtesy, pity, generosity, joy, which Caxton himself rightly saw as so strong an element in *Le Morte Darthur*. It is a joyous book as well as a tragic book, and we do Malory and ourselves an injustice if we do not give full credit to both elements. We may well follow the good and leave the evil, as Caxton recommends, recognising their co-existence in our experience.

V

FROM LOGRES TO CARBONEK: THE ARTHURIAD OF CHARLES WILLIAMS

Karl Heinz Göller

I

Among the modern poets of today, Charles Williams (1896-1945) has yet to receive the acknowledgement which he deserves, although he is one of the major shapers and re-makers of the Arthurian legend, as C. S. Lewis and others have pointed out.[1] Of course, Lewis' *Arthurian Torso* will always remain an indispensable guide through the labyrin-thine passages of the poet's work; and yet many paths remain to be explored.

In his incomplete prose work *The Figure of Arthur* Charles Williams delineates the intention of his poetic works *Taliessin Through Logres* and *Region of the Summer Stars.*[2] They

1. For engaging insights into the personal side of the poet, see James T. Como, ed., *C. S. Lewis at the Breakfast Table and other Remi-niscences* (New York, 1979); particularly the lively accounts of Derek S. Brewer, Erik Routley, Nathan C. Starr. No less vivid is the portrait sketched by Alice Mary Hadfield in her 'The Relationship of Charles Williams' Working Life to his Fiction', in *Shadows of the Imagin-ation: The Fantasies of C. S. Lewis, J. R. R. Tolkien, and Charles Williams*, ed. M. R. Hillegas (Carbondale, 1969; new ed. 1979). The Charles Williams Society of London, which was founded in 1975, issues a Newsletter with essential criticism and interpretation. Additional contributions are found in *Mythlore* (Los Angeles) which is devoted to Williams, Tolkien and Lewis. I particularly wish to express my appreciation to Martin Moynihan, Esq., who encouraged me to delve deeper into the mystic world of Charles Williams and who kindly brought me into contact with Mary Hadfield, one of the founder members of the Charles Williams Society.

2. Charles Williams, *Taliessin Through Logres* and *The Region of the Summer Stars* (London, 3rd ed. 1954). *Taliessin through Logres,*

are meant to portray the development of the legends of Arthur and the Grail, their gradual coalescence and fusion and the fate of the Grail world. Two subjects are of primary importance for Williams: the realm of King Arthur and that of the Grail. When these two focal points of Williams' *Arthuriad* are compared with medieval treatments — as for instance that of Malory, whose *Morte Darthur* can be regarded as one of Williams' main sources — the modern poet's originality becomes clear. The love story of Lancelot and Guinevere, which is perhaps the most appealing to modern audiences, is only allotted marginal treatment. The centre of the entire myth, and therewith the *raison d'être* of Williams' work, is clearly the Grail. The poet sees the union of the world of Arthur with that of the Grail less as a legendary or historical phenomenon, and far more as a complex symbol of the union of Empire and Christendom, that is to say as a symbol of the Ultimate Epiphany, the Second Advent of Christ.

Logres is the name Charles Williams gives to Arthur's realm in conformity with the Old French prose version.[3] It is a part or a province of the Byzantine Empire, which for Williams represented the incarnation of Divine Order. From the point

the Region of the Summer Stars by Charles Williams and Arthurian Torso by Charles Williams and C. S. Lewis, introd. by Mary Mc-Dermott Shideler (Grand Rapids, Michigan, 1974). Frequent use was made of Williams' most important work in prose on Arthurian mythology, *The Arthurian Torso*, as it was entitled by its editor, C. S. Lewis (London, 2nd ed. 1952). See also, his *The Image of the City and other Essays*, ed. Anne Ridler (London, 1958). A bibliography of secondary literature on Williams is to be found in John Heath-Stubbs, *Charles Williams*. Writers and their Work, No. 63 (London, 1955), 40-4. Additional mention must be made of Mary McDermott Shideler, *The Theology of Romantic Love. A Study in the Writings of Charles Williams* (New York, 1968), which includes a comprehensive bibliography of Williams' writing together with the reviews it received. Rev. by William V. Spanos in *JEGP*, 67 (1968), 719-22.

3. Logres as a name for the image of an ideal place and the destination of life's journey is analogous to St Augustine's New Jerusalem and Tolkien's True West. Cf. Jonnie Patricia Mobley, *Towards Logres: The Operation of Efficacious Grace in Novels by C. S. Lewis, Charles Williams, Muriel Spark, and Gabriel Fielding* (Diss., University of Southern California, 1973).

of view of medieval Arthurian romance, the Roman Empire would have been a more appropriate choice. But for Williams, Byzantium was connected to the idea of a strictly hierarchical power with an organic structure. Divine order was for him a matter of geometrical precision, with complete harmony of all the component parts. Rivalry of the member states of the Empire, or manifestations of national thought, did not fit into his conception.

Others besides Charles Williams used Byzantium as a symbolic vehicle, for example W. B. Yeats. Both were connected with the Golden Dawn Group of Chelsea occultists. The originality of Charles Williams lies in the utter Christianisation of the image; one might even say he baptized *goetia*.

One of the mystery writers of the Golden Dawn period, Arthur Machen, may have inspired Williams to the idea of a modern *parousia* symbolised by the grail. His story 'The Great Return' (1915) is an account of the Grail and its effect on a modern Welsh parish church. The idea of *perichoresis* or interpenetration may also have been suggested by one of Machen's stories.[4]

Thus Williams gives the story of King Arthur an entirely new slant. Its meaning can only be understood through a closer look at the development of earlier treatments of the Arthurian story. The idea of order already plays a prominent role in the *Historia Regum Britanniae* of Geoffrey of Monmouth.[5] The learned bishop of St Asaph is less interested in the heroic deeds of the historical King Arthur than in the idea of kingship, of which Arthur is a symbol. Geoffrey constructs a glorious past, in which Britain was a major power by reason of its unity and singleness of purpose, which enabled it to rival the Roman Empire. The historian's aim is the foundation of a political ideology, the creation and dissemination of the idea of an Anglo-Norman Empire. To this end he emphasises the *primordia urbis* and makes Arthur a figure

4. This I owe to a friendly communication of Martin Moynihan, Esq. Cf. *The Caerleon Edition of the Works of Arthur Machen*, 9 vols. (London, 1923), 'The Great Return', Vol.7, 191ff.

5. Editions: *The Historia Regum Britanniae of Geoffrey of Monmouth*, ed. A. Griscom (London and New York, 1929); *Historia Regum Britannaie, A Variant Version*, ed. J. Hammer (Cambridge, Mass., 1951).

larger than life, greater than Hector and Aeneas, Alexander and Charlemagne, a visible symbol of a realm which far surpassed that of the Romans in brilliance and in power. The foundation of the Empire sketched by Geoffrey was meant to lie beyond the reaches of the medieval *imperium*; his Arthur is meant as a negation of the uniqueness of the imperial office.[6]

In literary works after Geoffrey nationalist tendencies become more apparent,[7] and more emphasis is given to the conflict with Rome. The most complex Middle English treatment of the fate of King Arthur, the *Alliterative Morte Arthure*,[8] places the conflict with Rome at the focal point of the action. Even in the chronicles we can recognise a gradual shifting of interest in this direction.[9] In Geoffrey's history Arthur is about to climb the Alpine passes when the news of Mordred's treason reaches him, forcing a quick retreat. According to Peter of Langtoft[10] Arthur has already crossed the Alps and the trumpets in Pavia are announcing a feast,

6. On Geoffrey's intention, cf. W. F. Schirmer, *Die Frühen Darstellungen des Arthurstoffes* (Köln and Opladen, 1958), 19ff; further: Heinrich Pähler, *Strukturuntersuchungen zur Historia Regum Britanniae des Geoffrey of Monmouth* (Diss., Bonn, 1958), chapters 6 and 7.

7. The fact that Arthur was a mortal enemy of the Anglo-Saxons was gradually forgotten by Geoffrey's successors. Both Henry II and Edward I fought to suppress the troublesome legend of Arthur's return by having his body exhumed. A number of English kings liked to envision themselves in the rôle of *Arthurus redivivus*. The son of Henry VII was even baptized under the name of Arthur. On the legends of the Return, cf. R. S. Loomis, 'The Legend of Arthur's Survival', in *Arthurian Literature in the Middle Ages*, ed. R. S. Loomis (Oxford, 1959), 64-71.

8. Valerie Krishna, ed., *The Alliterative Morte Arthure. A Critical Edition* (New York, 1976). For a re-evaluation of this unique work see *The Alliterative Morte Arthure: A Reassessment of the Poem*, ed. Karl Heinz Göller (Woodbridge, 1981).

9. On the development of the figure of Arthur in historiography, cf. Herta Brandenburg, *Galfried von Monmouth und die frühmittelenglischen Chronisten* (Diss., Berlin, 1918).

10. *Chronicle of Peter of Langtoft*, 2 vols., ed. T. Wright (London, 1866-68).

when the bearer of bad tidings from Britain reaches Arthur. John Hardyng[11] places the final battle between Romans and Britains in the Toscana in central Italy. In the *Annals of Worcester*[12] which follow the *Liber de Compositione Castri Ambaziae*[13] in this respect, Arthur is forced to turn back shortly before reaching the city gates of Rome, where he hears about Mordred's betrayal. And finally Jean de Preis has Arthur marching into Rome in his *Mer des Histoires*,[14] and we see him crowned as Emperor. In a similar manner in the French prose version, as reflected in Sir Thomas Malory's *Morte Darthur*,[15] Arthur is crowned as emperor in Rome after a great victory over the Empire.

Charles Williams provides us with a completely different concept of the Arthurian myth. The major innovation consists in the exclusion of an antithetical opposition of *Logres* and Rome. Even in Tennyson's version, Rome was only the 'slowly fading mistress of the world'; the poet devotes one meagre sentence to the battle against Rome.[16] Williams saw the fight against the Roman emperor as a very unfortunate element of the Arthurian myth, and preferred to omit it. 'No national myth was ever the better for being set against a more universal authority', the poet tells us.[17] The result of dropping the rivalry between *Logres* and Rome is a denationalisation of the Arthurian myth. Arthur's realm is now an integral part of the Byzantine Empire.

The concept of organism is meant literally by Charles Williams. His point of departure is Wordsworth's idea that the

11. John Hardyng, *The Chronicle, Together with the Continuations by R. Grafton*, ed. H. Ellis (London, 1812).

12. *Annales de Wigornia*, in *Annales Monastici IV*, ed. H. R. Luard, Rolls Series (London, 1869).

13. *Liber de Compositione Castri Ambaziae*, in *Chroniques des Comtes d'Anjou*, ed. P. Marchegay and A. Salmon (Paris, 1871).

14. *Mer des Histoires*, in *Chroniques Belges*, 6 vols., ed. A. Borgnet, S. Bormans, Belgian Royal Academy (Brussels, 1864-80).

15. *The Works of Sir Thomas Malory*, ed. Eugène Vinaver (London, 2nd ed., 1967).

16. 'The Coming of Arthur', in A. Tennyson, *Poetical Works* (London, 1954), 295.

17. *Arthurian Torso*, 83.

human body is an index of a greater universal order – the old medieval topos of microcosm and macrocosm.[18] The words which appear in an index also appear in the corresponding text, and in a similar manner the qualities and the structural features of the human body are found in counterpart in the universe. The Empire of *Logres* is conceived as an analogy to the human body. The head is *Logres*, for the historical source of the myth lies in Britain; it gains consciousness here and is given verbal form.[19] The breasts are the country of France, which fed Christendom with the milk of knowledge and of faith ('the breasts of *intelligo* and *credo*').[20] Rome is represented through the hands of the Pope, which convey the blessing of the Church to the faithful. The navel stands for Byzantium, the organic centre and seat of the Empire; the loins are Jerusalem, where Christ was crucified and the new Adam born.[21] Thus the Empire is seen as an organism, and the human body, in turn, as a mirror of the Empire, the Kingdom of God.[22]

Beyond this Empire to the South is *P'o-l'u*, the land of the Antipodes, where order dissolves into anarchy. Octopi with giant tentacles creep over the slimy sea and stare with lidless

18. Cf. 'The Index of the Body', *The Image of the City*, 80-7.

19. Cf. J. Heath-Stubbs, *Charles Williams*, 36.

20. *Taliessin Through Logres*, 8.

21. In regard to Jerusalem as the site of Christ's crucifixion and the birth-place of the New Adam, one can ask whether Williams was familiar with the ancient Omphalos concept; cf. Arno Esch, 'Paradise and Calvary', *Anglia*, 78 (1960), 74-7.

22. *Arthurian Torso*, 107-8. As source for Williams' geographical myth, Dante, among others, must be mentioned, who saw Jerusalem as the centre of civilized earth. But even more significant is the poetic geography found in Blake, and the symbolic meaning he saw in the four directions – North, South, East and West. The various *states* correspond to parts of Williams' anatomical myth. Cf. Maung Ba-Han, *William Blake: His Mysticism* (Bordeaux, 1924), 78: 'They (the four "states") are sometimes spoken of as "the four worlds of humanity in every man" ... and sometimes personified as the "four mighty ones ... in every man". They are designated the four "Zoas" or "Lifes" in Eternity, and their names are Urthona (or Los), Urizen, Luvah and Tharmas. The Directions of their seats "in eternal times" were respectively North, South, East and West.'

eyes at the coast of the Empire. Images from Coleridge's *Ancient Mariner* and Wells' *War of the Worlds* blend with the medieval concept of the Antipodes, which interestingly enough were seen as a negative counterpart of the Arthurian world in the *Draco Normannicus* of Etienne de Rouen.[23]

P'o-l'u is a kind of Hell, the sphere of power of the Headless Emperor. To the West of *Logres* lies *Broceliande*,[24] the mysterious world of making and shaping, of the *Apeiron*. The mistress of this forest is Nimue. She appears in mortal guise, but as the 'Mother of Making' she combines earthly existence with the transcendent. Nimue's children are Merlin and Brisen, perceptible and active embodiments of time and space. In the forest of *Broceliande*, beyond the borders of the Empire, stands the castle of *Carbonek* where the Grail and the Bleeding Lance are kept. Merlin and Brisen are preparing the union of Byzantium and *Carbonek*, the welding of the worldly and religious ideals, the perfection of Christendom on earth — namely the *parousia*.

Logres, which medieval authors did not localize geographically, has become a spiritual landscape in the writings of Charles Williams, one whose main characteristic is geometrical order. But order is not seen as a value in itself, rather, it stands as a sign for the sacred, directing us to God, the operation of whose Providence is revealed in the harmony of mathematical and geometrical symbols. According to Williams, religion is to be expressed in terms of mathematical clarity, whose contours are clearly visible. Sin is seen accordingly as the destruction of an ordered pattern or structure, the derangement of God's plans through man.[25]

Logres with its hierarchical order and rationality thus refers to an ordered universe, for which it can stand as an index in the same way as the human body stands for the Empire. But *Logres* is only a passing realization of an ideal society, the creation of a happy moment in time, and thus

23. *The Draco Normannicus of Etienne de Rouen*, ed. R. Howlett, Rolls Series (London, 1885).

24. On Broceliande, cf. McDermott Shideler, *The Theology of Romantic Love*, 102ff.

25. Cf. *The Image of the City*, 145; as well as, Charles Moorman, *Arthurian Triptych, Mythic Materials in Charles Williams, C. S. Lewis and T. S. Eliot* (New York, 1960), 67.

vulnerable and instable. It is dependent upon human co-operation with the overall plan. When selfless love is lacking and man makes himself the centre of this world, chaos breaks in: 'Things fall apart, the centre cannot hold'.[26]

Compared with Malory's account of the dissolution of the Round Table and of the Arthurian world, that is to say the destruction of secular power, the dimensions have been expanded by Williams. They remind us of Milton and of his representation of the fall of mankind.[27] Heaven and earth are joined in a new mythic kingdom which is by no means unreal because it lacks historical existence, nor is it merely an archetypical description of an utopian *Phantastikón*. It is far more a representation of man's situation in this world, and therefore of universal validity even for modern man. Besides its historical applicability, the myth shaped by Williams has a life of its own, and this is what gives it meaning and depth.

In much the same way as he transforms the world of King Arthur, Williams also presents the world of the Grail in a form not previously found in English literature. Perhaps we could say that the legend of the Grail had never been given adequate poetic treatment in English literature before Charles Williams. Besides the insignificant work of Henry Lovelich,[28] there are five further English treatments of the early history of the Grail which must already have been known in England by 1250, as an interpolation in *De Antiquitate Glastoniensis*

---

26. William Butler Yeats, 'The Second Coming', in *The Collected Poems* (London, 1958), 211.

27. Cf. Nathan Comfort Starr, *King Arthur Today: The Arthurian Legend in English and American Literature 1901-1953* (Gainesville, 1954), 178.

28. *The History of the Holy Grail*, by Henry Lovelich, skynner, ed. F. J. Furnivall, EETS ES 20/24, 28/30 (London, 1874-78); Dorothy Kempe, *The Legend of the Holy Grail, its Sources, Character and Development* ('Introduction' to, and Part V of Henry Lovelich's Verse 'History of the Holy Grail') (London, 1905). This work, which dates back to 1430, is a translation of the French *Estoire del Saint Graal* without any additions or alterations whatsoever. In fact, the language is so stiff and halting, and the treatment so little suited to the elevated nature of the topic, that we sympathize with the wry remark of the editor that Lovelich must have felt unfulfilled by his trade as a furrier.

Ecclesiae[29] shows. The oldest of the versions which have been preserved is a fragment contained in the alliterative poem *Joseph of Arimathia*.[30] The *Queste del Saint Graal*,[31] however, is only found in English in Thomas Malory's *Morte Darthur*,[32] which Charles Williams evidently used as a major source.

Malory had little sympathy for the secret of the Grail and its mystic function.[33] Spiritual knighthood was far less important to him than worldly glory and honour. And yet it is not necessarily a contradiction that his entire account of the Quest follows his sources more closely than the remaining parts of his work. He adopts only the matter (*matière*), while at the same time changing the *sens* entirely. The transcendental goal of the Quest was meant to direct the knight away from his entanglement in the earthly code of honour towards the true purpose of life. Malory, however, makes the Grail an

29. *William of Malmesbury, Liber de Antiquitate Glastoniensis Ecclesiae*, in J. P. Migne, *Patrologia Latina*, Vol.179, cols. 1682-1734.

30. *Joseph of Arimathia*, ed. W. W. Skeat, EETS OS 44 (London, 1871).

31. On the background of the Quest of the Grail, see Loomis, *Arthurian Literature*, esp. R. S. Loomis, 'The Origin of the Grail Legends", 274-294; Jean Frappier, 'The Vulgate Cycle", 295-318; Fanni Bogdanow, 'The *Suite du Merlin* and the Post-Vulgate *Roman du Graal*", 325-335.

32. In his account of the Quest of the Grail, Malory follows the Old French prose version, which seems to have been of monastic origin, at least for this part. The hermit who interprets the hierarchy of virtues places Chastity and Virginity at the height of the scale, a surprising turn-about-face after Courtly Love has just been explained as the main inspiration and code of behaviour of knighthood and Chivalry. Virginity is followed in descending order by Humility, Patience, Righteousness, and Love. During the Vigil before Whitsunday, the tables in Arthur's hall are placed in the same position prescribed for this feast in the Rule of Citeaux. In addition, the central problem of the nature of Grace and the repeated discussions of Trans-substantiation give rise to the idea that the author must have been a Cistercian monk. Cf. Loomis, *Arthurian Literature*, 306.

33. Cf. E. Vinaver, *The Works of Sir Thomas Malory*, I, 70ff.

integral part of his world of knighthood,[34] a fact which Williams seems to have overlooked. The hierarchical world of values of the French prose version culminates in Galahad, a saintly Christ-like figure, from whom even adventures retreat to allow him free passage. Although he belongs to the court of Arthur and to the Round Table, his true home and destiny is the mythic Sarras, and in place of jousting and tournaments his mission is the Grail. And yet the French author never doubts the fact that Galahad is the best knight in the world, far better than all the others. Malory, however, in sharp contrast to his sources, insists on the fact that Lancelot was a better knight than his son Galahad. In this way Malory has basically secularized his source. Through the figure of Lancelot he places spiritual knighthood on an equal footing with secular knighthood. The Quest becomes one knightly adventure among many others.[35]

Malory's attitude towards the Quest of the Grail is by no means to be seen as the failing of an individual author who is far too earth-bound. On the contrary, such a reaction to the Quest of the Grail seems to be widespread, even today, in England and everywhere else in the world. The Grail seems to have become a stumbling stone for modern man, who is no longer capable of appreciating the ascetic ideal of life. John W. Donaldson, one of the more recent editors of Malory, has thus omitted the Quest entirely. He justifies this step by pointing out that this part of the story evidently stems from monastic interpolation and cannot be reconciled with the spirit of knighthood. In his eyes, the ideals of chastity and

34. This is particularly easy to demonstrate in the case of Lancelot, Malory's explicit favourite and, as in the French version, still 'le meilleur chevalier du monde'. Naturally as such he had to be excluded from the Quest. Malory had already portrayed his adulterous love for Guinevere, thus stamping Lancelot as sinful and unworthy of the vision of the Grail.

35. The somewhat neglected tale of the healing of Knight Urry is revealing on this point. Lancelot cures him merely by the laying on of hands and by prayer, an incident inserted by Malory without an apparent source. As in his account of the Quest, Malory has elevated the rôle of earthly knighthood here. Cf. P. E. Tucker, 'A Source for "The Healing of Sir Urry" in the "Morte Darthur"', *MLR*, 50 (1955), 490-2.

atonement are completely foreign elements, alien to the tenor of the narrative. Donaldson's conclusion is that this leads to completely false conceptions of Arthur and his knights.[36] In a similar manner, Tennyson had portrayed the Quest of the Grail as the adventure of the three mystics Galahad, Perceval and Bors, one which was instigated by the ecstatic visions of holy virgins. The Round Table, and with it common man, had no part in the Grail.[37]

Charles Williams is acquainted with such ideas. He has Mordred, the traitor and cynic, say: 'My father often thought about the value of the Grail for his salvation; but I can do without such fairy mechanisms. Should something like the Grail really exist, which is hardly likely, I shall send a dozen of my knights in order to destroy it.'[38]

For Williams, the Grail is no theatrical prop, but rather a tangible spiritual power. A large portion of his later poetry is aimed at restoring the Grail to its proper position, an undertaking which was certainly courageous, if not very promising.

Williams goes about his task as a scholar and a poet. His prose work *The Figure of Arthur* shows an astounding knowledge of the nearly overwhelming store of Arthurian secondary literature. His hypothesis on the origin of the Grail is unequivocal and, it must be admitted, reveals a certain amount of prejudice. Whether the Grail be a chalice or a bowl or some other kind of vessel, its first appearance in European literature is bound up with the Sacred Host. Chrétien's Grail has no connection with the Celtic fairy-tale vessel or Cauldron of Plenty. It provides food not for the body, but for the soul. Thus Williams regards the Grail as a ciborium containing the Holy Bread of the Eucharist.[39] In contrast to the versions of Malory and Tennyson, it does not serve a small elite, but is destined for all mankind.

Williams sees the wound of the Fisher-King as a physical

---

36. *Arthur Pendragon of Britain* (New York, 1943).

37. 'The Holy Grail', in A. Tennyson, *Poetical Works*, 401.

38. 'The Meditation of Mordred', in *The Region of the Summer Stars*, 47-9, here 48.

39. According to Chrétien, however, the Grail is a vessel for food in which common salmon and lampreys are served, and thus its transformation from a profane object to a sacred one in the form of a chalice or ciborium is a phenomenon that remains to be explained.

and spiritual hurt suffered by the entire human race. Naturally he does not ignore the sexual connotations of the wound; but he places them in proper perspective by viewing them in terms of their symbolic and allegorical value. The reader acquainted with his poems is led immediately to think of Jerusalem and its significance in the myth of the organic body, an analogy which provides a deeper understanding of what happens in the Castle of the Grail.[40]

Perceval's failure is attributed by Williams to an inner feeling of guilt which forbids him to approach the sanctuary. The reason first given by Chrétien — respect for the advice of Gournemant — is disregarded by Williams as being too minor. Perceval's guilt is far more to be seen in his cruel impatience towards his mother, in a natural, unreflected and unholy impulse, in short: in natural sin.

Williams goes on to treat the various continuations of Chrétien's unfinished narrative, whose main contribution to the legend of the Grail lies in the combination and sublimation of images already present. The combination of the Grail and the Bleeding Lance with Christian tradition is clearly evident in these authors, as well as the great benefit which Perceval's question might have meant for the country. A new element is to be seen in the introduction of the Waste Land motif to the myth, a concept originally pagan, according to which natural fertility is dependent upon the sexual potency of the ruler. The wound of the Fisher-King is explained by the Dolorous Blow of the sword, which gains supreme importance in Williams' new version of the myth as a symbol of original sin. Williams attributes similar importance to the visit of the entire Round Table to the Grail Castle on the occasion of Perceval's coronation. Here we see an Arthur-

40. In regard to the Grail and Bleeding Lance, Williams points out that they appear for the first time in this form in Chrétien. There were Celtic lances which blazed lightning and fire, but not one that bled. One cannot blame Williams for not finding the reason for the new image. Of course, Chrétien has a different lance in mind in the procession than the one that wounded the king. Thus the bleeding of the spear, and the healing of the wound with the blood of the spear must be explained. Williams has evidently thought of the lance of Longinus which pierced the side of Christ in this connection, in the context of his discussion of the *Conte du Graal*.

ian world given a dynamic orientation towards a new spiritual centre.

The last version of the Grail story discussed by Williams is *Perlesvaus*. It is easy to see why Williams took such an interest in this particular work. Its exposition conveys the impression that Arthur and the Grail are to be combined in a single story. In order to restore his lost reputation, Arthur rides through the land in search of adventure. In the chapel of a hermitage he experiences the mystery of the Eucharist. He has a vision of a beautiful woman on the altar with a child upon her knee. While the Hermit celebrates Mass, the child is transformed into the Man of Sorrows with a crown of thorns upon his head. Arthur sees himself in this figure, and pity draws tears to his eyes. Immediately Christ is retransformed into the child, and with the *ite missa est* the vision and the light which framed it are extinguished. Full of new resolutions, Arthur returns to Cardoil and promises Guinevere that he will do the will of God from that time onward.

At this point, according to Williams, Arthur has come as close to the mystery as he ever will. In no other version is the king accorded such measure of grace, with the exception perhaps of Galahad's appearance at the royal court in Malory. A fusion of the two worlds, however, does not take place. The world of the Grail and the Arthurian world hardly come in contact in *Perlesvaus*. Williams, however, saw the combination of these two subjects as his major task.

II

The poem on the calling of Taliessin to his vocation is contained in the volume of poetry entitled *The Region of the Summer Stars*, which for the most part was composed later than the poems in the previous volume *Taliessin Through Logres*. Both taken together compose the Arthuriad of Williams: '. . . in general the argument of the series is the expectation of the return of Our Lord by means of the Grail and the establishment of the kingdom of Logres (or Britain) to this end by the powers of the Empire and Broceliande.' [41]

41. *The Region of the Summer Stars*, 'Preface', vii.

According to the chronology of the Arthurian kingdom, the 'Calling of Taliessin' forms the beginning of the cycle. Here the poet and seer Taliessin[42] learns in a dream vision of the establishment of the Kingdom of Logres in which he is to play a part. It is true that he cannot understand the full connotations of his task because he is still too much involved in the druidism and magic lore of his native land; and yet he is faintly aware of the greatness of his mission, the enormous appeal of the ideas of Byzantium and of the Grail. On the other hand, he also sees the possibility of the fall of Logres, even if it is only a vague premonition. Thus at the very beginning of Taliessin's way to Byzantium, the fate of Arthur's realm is foreshadowed.

The poem *The Calling of Taliessin* begins in the style of the *Mabinogion* with the description of the origin of Taliessin. No one knows from whom the poet and seer is descended. The beginnings of poetry and prophecy are veiled in clouded darkness. But already the discovery of the infant Taliessin in a weir of the River Wye is a kind of sign for everything that is to follow. Subtle associations and the use of anticipation and innuendo recall biblical parallels, many of them barely noticeable for the reader at first and only fully understandable after the whole has been read. Taliessin is carried down

42. The historical Taliessin lived in the sixth century, and the poetry attributed to him has been preserved in the *Book of Taliessin* (c.1275). Twelve historical poems from this collection date back to the sixth century and are regarded by Celtic scholars as 'the genuine work of Taliessin'. Cf. A. L. Owen, *The Famous Druids* (Oxford, 1962), 201ff. Lady Charlotte Guest translated the story of Taliessin in her *Mabinogion*. The following passage quoted from the translation ('Taliessin', in *The Mabinogion*, transl. by Lady Charlotte Guest (London, 1877), 471-94) casts helpful light on our poem:

And my original country is the region of the summer stars; . . .
I was with my Lord in the highest sphere,
On the fall of Lucifer into the depth of hell:
I have borne a banner before Alexander; . . .
I have been loquacious prior to being gifted with speech; . . .
I am able to instruct the whole universe.
I shall be until the day of doom on the face of the earth;
And it is not known whether my body is flesh or fish.

(pp.482-3)

the river in a willow basket covered with leather, and is brought to land by King Elphin. He is thus comparable to the Hebrew *Mosheh*, for this name means: one drawn out of the water. What Moses was for the people of the Jews, Taliessin is to become for Logres and for Britain.

King Elphin is rooted in paganism and the bloody handiwork of war; his connection with poetry is limited to a hearty song after the feast. And nevertheless he accepts the gift of the river, and the child has already begun to sing: on the druidic lore of reincarnation, on the preordained law of transformation whose circle begins with fish and ends again with fish, namely: '. . . from shapes that eat / to shapes that are eaten, and then to the fish split / to be at once on the dish and again in the sea'.[43]

This law of Karma rules Taliessin, and with him the entire pagan world; for God has not yet led them into the land of the Trinity and set them free. And yet as much as this senseless movement back to the point of departure might seem a closed circle, it is rather a sign of something new and final, the perfection of the cycle of destiny and therewith the liberation and emancipation of the individual. Bread and fish recall the mystery of the Eucharist of which Williams says: '. . . they were eaten, yet they themselves received the eater into themselves; they were separate, yet they were one.'[44] This is almost certainly the antitype of the 'shapes that eat / to shapes that are eaten'. The metamorphosis which takes place under the law of Karma as a historical or mythical reality serves at the same time as a prototype, which is later fulfilled in the Christian Empire of Byzantium. The mystic sense of the pagan world is to be seen in such prototypes, which foreshadow the Empire to come, even if it is only in the unconscious song of a poet who has not yet attained maturity as a prophet.

The account of Taliessin's childhood and youth is likewise full of allusion, anticipation and connotation. It is Williams'

---

43. *The Region of the Summer Stars*, 6; cf. on Celtic concepts of reincarnation: Jan de Vries, *Keltische Religion* (Stuttgart, 1961), 252.

44. *Arthurian Torso*, 22; on the earlier tradition of Taliessin, cf. Owen, *Famous Druids*, 213.

myth of the rise of poetic genius.[45] Again we have an interlacing of various threads, motifs and types of the poetic
message; the individual tones of the son echo in a chord of
exotic harmony. The point of departure is the Celtic image of
the Cauldron of Ceridwen, from which the art of poetry spills
forth. Superimposed upon this, however, is a kind of cosmic
story of the Muse whose origins are unknown. Taliessin was
already at the Throne of God when the world was created.
His spirit moved over the waters during the flood, and it
ascended into the third heaven, his true home, where the
summer stars shine – symbols of the eternal ideas. Here we
hear an echo of William Blake's *Songs of Experience*: 'Hear
the voice of the bard, who Present, Past and Future sees', and
yet there is a clearly Christian accent. Although he has not yet
found the formula of the Empire, the pillar of Christianity,
Taliessin has a premonition of the coming liberation from the
cycle of destiny, although, for the time being, merely in the
form of vague correspondences and similarities.

Taliessin lives not only on a physical plane, but also in the
poetic breath of the spirit, and life and knowledge coalesce in
the trinity of verse, again a typological image which creates
anticipation in the poem and sets a new pole, a new focal
centre for the action and for the thoughts of the reader: 'I
was thrall to Ceridwen and free in the manger of an ass'[46] –
mysterious connotations of Bethlehem and the salvation and
rebirth of mankind. Thus the personality of the poet comes
into focus as the individual vessel of the Muse who transforms
man, makes him a tool and thereby raises him above his kind.
At the same time, however, she makes the poet a chimera,
neither fish nor fowl, so terribly divided from other men that
no woman can love him, a man still heard by scholars but no
longer heeded, a man closer to the dead than to the living.

The Empire (and here this means Christendom) is at first
unknown to Taliessin, save in the form of mysterious and
vague allusions. Minor external objects are explained to him,
the pantry of the monks, the bread and beans of the hermits,

45. In what follows, Williams, in my opinion, failed to distinguish
clearly enough between bards, *vates*, and Druids. The Celtic priest-
hood fulfilled several functions which can no longer be clearly
separated today. Cf. Jan de Vries, *Keltische Religion*, 216-7.

46. *The Region of the Summer Stars*, 7.

the outer shells of symbols whose significance Taliessin senses because he knows the laws of correspondence. But one day he learns of the Kingdom of God and of its history on earth, of the original sin of Adam and the salvation of mankind through Christ, whose unbelievable, all-comprehending love transformed the tree of Adam into the cross of crucifixion. According to an early Christian legend, Paradise and Mount Calvary were both located in the same place, called *medium terrae*.[47] This is where creation began, and here Adam was born and reborn. And the wood of the cross, according to the same legend, was that of the tree of Adam. The message which reaches Taliessin is only fragmentary and vague, but nevertheless it suffices to make everything he has heard so far appear black and white magic (*goety*, black magic and *theurgy*, white magic). Even the poetry of the pagan world appears shabby in comparison with the shadowy dream of the Empire, whose component parts materialize from the imagination of the poet, take on the semblance of a human body, a microcosm which mirrors in itself all aspects of the Empire. The seed has been sown in Taliessin's heart. His thirst has been awakened for the metaphysics of salvation. He wants to learn more about it than he can gather on the River Wye. For this reason he departs for Byzantium, the image of the City of God.

Taliessin's way leads him along the western coast of England towards the Channel. On his left lies the waste land that is one day to become Logres, and on his right the wood and the sea of Broceliande, the mysterious realm of making, the *Apeiron*, home of Nimue who shapes all earthly things according to their celestial ideas. Beyond Broceliande lies the castle of the Grail, and beyond that the holy land of Sarras. Broceliande is borderland, the realm between the here and the beyond, and thus known only to the elect. No one returns unchanged from this land — some come again as saints, others as empty-headed prattlers who unashamedly preach their metaphysics as if it were gospel. Taliessin only passes through the outer fringes of the wood, and yet his soul is seized by fear and doubt. In the face of the monumental

47. *The Book of the Cave of Treasures*, transl. from the Syriac Text of the British Museum MS. Add. 25875 by Sir E. A. Wallis Budge (London, 1927), 63; cf. also n. 21, Esch.

task which lies before him he very nearly despairs: 'dividing word from thing and uniting thing to word', that is the separation of the word or concept from the archetypes of celestial truths, and the fusion of these words with their natural objects on Earth in poetic images and symbols.

While he waits, trying to gather himself, he is approached by a shining form which divides into two parts, and becomes a man and a woman — Merlin and Brisen, 'time and space, duration and extension'. They come from Broceliande and intend to establish a kingdom in Logres in which Byzantium and Broceliande will be united. We hear about the kingdom for the first time in this passage, and we know no more than Taliessin what it is all about. But like the poet we sense that in Logres the divine mystery will take form, that the creation of the perfect man is to take place. Taliessin is not granted more knowledge than that. He must be happy if his spirit can comprehend the space which divides him from Carbonek. He is not allowed to enquire after Sarras, for he has not yet been to Byzantium and is thus still in the stage of the Druid poet who can sense parallels and analogies but is earth-bound by nature and cannot yet participate in the *Feeling Intellect*.

With a cosmic image of sublime beauty, Williams introduces the mysterious magic of Merlin and Brisen. The day draws to a close, the sun sinks to the Antipodes, and the Earth casts its conic shadow into space.[48]

This image is taken from the *Divine Comedy, Paradiso* IX. 118.[49] According to Dante's view (indeed according to medieval astronomy in general), the universe is entirely lighted by the sun. Night is caused by the cone-shaped shadow cast by the Earth. Because the Earth stands at the centre of the universe and the sun revolves around it, we must imagine Earth's shadow moving like the rotating hand of a clock.[50] It reaches no further than the sphere of Venus, thus darkening only the inner planetary heavens, whose spheres according to

48. On the imagery of the shadow, cf. Carl Dee Dockery, *The Myth of the Shadow in the Fantasies of Williams, Lewis and Tolkien* (Diss., Auburn University, 1975).

49. Cf. the useful commentary on Dante's concept of the universe in *The Divine Comedy of Dante Alighieri*, introd. by C. H. Grandgent, trans, by J. A. Carlyle and P. H. Wicksteed (New York, 1944).

50. Cf. C. S. Lewis, *The Discarded Image* (Cambridge, 1964), 111-2.

Dante symbolize the lower levels of imperfect holiness still tinged with earthliness. Williams likewise allows the point of the cone to reach the sphere of Venus, but at this point the image loses its concrete form and dissolves into an abstract concept. The third heaven, as Williams emphasises, is non-spatial: this must definitely be seen as a conscious device of the poet, who always takes the material world as his point of departure, only to pass over to the abstract ideal. In the case in question, the reader is additionally struck by the suspicion that the medieval model of the universe composed of spheres with the Earth at its centre must, for obvious reasons, be disguised. For naturally Williams knew that Earth's shadow could not fall in the sphere of Venus, which is nearer to the sun than the Earth.

The transformation of the image into an abstract one distracts from the geocentrical orientation of the model which forms the basis for Williams' thought and poetry. This becomes particularly clear in *The Coming of Galahad*. In *The Calling of Taliessin*, Williams was less concerned with the idea of an ordered universe, than with the opposition between idea and reality. For him the third heaven is the non-spatial home of likewise non-spatial ideas, according to whose arche-types Nimue creates objects and living beings on Earth. The sphere of Venus is transformed into a Platonic realm of celestial love and beauty, and the light of the ideas which have their home here is seen when the sun sinks, and all earthly things, the images of the ideas, are cast into invisibility. This is when Merlin and Brisen are able to hear the activity of the *Feeling Intellect* as a faint humming at the point of the conic shadow, a sign of the coming establishment of Logres and the advent of Sarras.

Taliessin does not understand the magic formula itself, and he experiences it only half-consciously as within a dream. Fate is determined by space and time (Brisen and Merlin), and the seer can only perceive it and portray it. Merlin marks the magic pentagram on the floor, the Druidic sign which was regarded as a symbol of perfection by the Platonists, Pythagoreans and Gnostics. Under Merlin's hands the flames of potential intellect rise up, and much in the same way as the shadow of Earth falls into space, reaching the third heaven, and darkness renders the ideas visible, so the shadow of Brisen falls upon Logres, which is still waste land waiting

139

for the advent of Sarras. The images of celestial ideas are not yet evident.

Only the accidentals of the magic act sink into Taliessin's heart. He does not yet understand the substance of the magic. And yet its connotations suffice to give him an idea of the sequence of coming events and his own mission. At first he only sees Brisen's back: she stares into the fire as if in a hypnotic trance. The flames throw red signs on her back, which for Taliessin is slowly transformed into snow-covered mountains – as can only happen in a dream. At first he sees the mountains in the ruby light of the fire, then the dreamer sees green meadows and steep mountain passes, and he sees himself as a wanderer in this landscape. He crosses the Apennine Mountains, and sails across the Caspian Sea in a storm. Brisen's back thus becomes a landscape in the dream of the poet, a world which as a macrocosm contains all the counterparts of the qualities and features of the human body, which can serve as an index for it. Each part of the land must be sought out by Taliessin in his search for wisdom.

Suddenly and unexpectedly a city is seen on the coast, bright and lovely beyond words, illuminated by rays of a mystic sun. Both city and light lie beyond the reach of Taliessin's dream. Poetry cannot reach that far, not even in a dream. Shortly before the final goal, the shining ray of glory is hidden from the poet by a cloud and becomes again the back of Brisen, which Williams calls 'recapitulatory'. Again the focus shifts from Brisen's back to the shadows that fall on Logres, and now Taliessin sees the stones in the waste land burst into light and shine like the summer stars – hope and anticipation of the fruitful union of Carbonek and Caerleon.

Taliessin, entangled in the pagan codex of the purely factual, can only take part in Merlin's magic through the medium of a dream vision. And yet from accidental details the seer and the reader are able to gain a glimpse of the Empire. The metamorphosis of the images takes place with dreamlike ease, and transitions, as in dreams, are often motivated by a single feature, such as the ruby colour of the fire as a *tertium comparationis* to completely unrelated and unvisualised objects, which develop according to a law of their own from images already present. Brisen's back becomes a snow-covered mountain, the Apennines, the Caspian Sea at the foot of the Caucasus, and once again the body of Brisen. The light of the magic flame in the pentagram is transformed to firelight on the snow-covered mountains, to the light of Sarras which originates from suns beyond the sun, then becomes the shining glory of deepest truth, and once again is transformed back to the gentle flickering fire of Merlin.

And yet we never have the impression that metaphors are manipulated at will; indeed there is never the slightest suspicion of intentional vagueness and mysteriousness on the side of the poet. The key image, that of the 'recapitulatory body', acts as an aid towards easy comprehension of the poetic message, which does not attempt more clarity for the simple reason that it is not based on facts or logical concepts, but rather on visionary premonitions.

Although the summer stars disappear the next morning with the dawning of light, the world (Logres) has changed. Dawn is seen in the rosy hue of porphyry, like the imperial stairway, the womb of woman, or the *largesse* of the emperor. And yet, for a short while, there is a new focal point in Logres, the eye of the storm which has devoured all the summer stars, as tiny as can be, but lit from within like the egg of a glow-worm. It is the light of the three-fold Trinity, the symbol of the task now given to Taliessin by Merlin: go to Byzantium! Taliessin hears and understands Merlin. His eyes fall on Brisen, and again her shadow is transformed, this time to an immense monumental stairway which leads from the brain (Logres) down to the base (Broceliande). The way from the Forest of Making and Shaping to Camelot is free. Above all, however, Carbonek can now be brought to Logres, and thus the king awaits the advent of the Trinity on the topmost peak of the stairway.

The idea that the salvation and perfection of mankind should take place in Britain is not a private mythology of Williams, but has a long history of development.[51] In the words of William Blake, who is spiritually very much akin to Charles Williams, we read in *Jerusalem* (pl. 27): 'All things Begin and End in Albions Ancient Druid Rocky Shore . . . You have a tradition, that Man anciently containd in his mighty limbs all things in Heaven and Earth: this you received (*sic*) from the Druids. But now the Starry Heavens

---

51. Cf. C. C. Dobson, *Did Our Lord Visit Britain?* (Glastonbury, 7th ed., 1958).

are fled from the mighty limbs of Albion'.[52] According to Blake, Jerusalem is the emanation of the giant Albion, and Britain the first home of patriarchal religion, and therefore the original Holy Land.

Taliessin sees himself as a poet and singer at the foot of the throne of the Dragon. The entire court stares out upon the sea and sees a ship, apparently from Sarras, carrying the Grail which rests in the hands of Helayne, the daughter of the Grail king. In order not to divulge the secret, Williams uses the device of a dream within a dream: Taliessin finds himself suddenly aboard ship; and there, in a state of ecstasy, he senses the nature of the object concealed under the saffron-yellow cloth. Shortly after this, however, his limbs lose their stiffness, and still caught up in the dream he sees himself in the magic pentagram. The stairway gradually disappears from sight, and those that stood at its top fly into empty space together with the throne of the Dragon – a psychologically subtle, even superb account of gradual awakening from a deep dream.

Taliessin appears to be unable to detach himself from the vision. He is still caught up in it, but his intellect cannot encompass its imaginative world. He dozes in half-consciousness, and again he receives Merlin's command: son of the bard, go to Byzantium! He and Brisen have already taken the possible failure of the Empire into account, and have consequently kept their rite ambivalent. Already there is a gentle undertone of approaching catastrophe, the first signs of disaster, namely the downfall of Logres, which cannot come up to the demanding task. And yet Merlin has taken precautions against even this eventuality. Taliessin will lead his followers in Logres along the same spiritual paths marked by Galahad, the chosen one of the Grail. This concludes the poem, and each one goes his way: Brisen to Carbonek, Merlin to Camelot and Taliessin to Byzantium.

The spiritual tension of the poem is marked by the poles of light and darkness. But they do not form a simple symbolic equation: light for truth and wisdom, and darkness for falsehood and ignorance. On the contrary, the light of the idea can only shine when it has become dark on Earth, when the

52. G. E. Bentley, ed., *William Blake's Writings*, 2 vols. (Oxford, 1978), I, 470.

hard and sober light of the sun, which Williams (like Words-worth) associates with the negative connotations of human *ratio*, has been extinguished, when a shadow is cast on the object of perception, thus enabling it to shine of its own accord. Paradoxically, it is Earth itself which casts its shadow upon things and into space, thus enabling the summer stars of the ideas to shine. The concrete image of Earth and its spatial extension is Brisen. Her shadow falls upon Logres, and the land which is at first dark begins to shine in a reflection of the stars mirrored again in the waste land — an earthly equivalent of the cosmic darkening of space through the conic shadow of Earth, and of the shining of the summer stars which is thereby made possible.

Alongside this polarity, and at the same time inter-penetration of light and darkness, we find the image of the waste land, a key symbol for both Charles Williams and T.S. Eliot. Logres has not yet achieved the state of perfect order. It is not lack of water which makes the land a waste land, nor sterility and infertility, but rather the anarchy of civil war, the lack of law and order. Logres is still wilderness, it has not yet taken on the form of *res publica*, for its members are still in a state of strife. Automatically the reader thinks of: 'Omne regnum in se ipsum divisum desolabitur'.[53] Waste land for Williams means egotism, isolation and autonomy expressed through the image of barter or communication made impossible. The opposite pole is represented by the harmoni-ous integration of the individual in the greater organic whole. Such an integration is only possible by means of *largesse* and exchange, concretely symbolised by the wagon and the ship at the Golden Horn, by human interaction and exchange. The in-dividual states and kingdoms are not autonomous; they belong together in the same way that the limbs and organs of the body do, and what connects them with one another is *largesse* and exchange. But this is not presented to us as a general principle; it is demonstrated in an exemplary way by Taliessin, who, before he can learn to think in Merlin's style, must first travel many miles through the Empire. Only 'ranging the themes', that is to say, travelling through the provinces of the Empire, will lead him to comprehend the organic unity of the world, and enable him to fulfil his rôle in it.

53. Luke 11.17.

The image of the waste land is connected with the idea of Advent. Logres and the world await salvation on the border of Broceliande and Sarras, whence the Trinity is to come. The Grail carried by Helayne is a symbol of Divine Love, which is to bring about the birth of perfect man on earth. It is the symbol of *parousia*, the Second Advent of Christ, and therewith of God's Kingdom on earth.

Taliessin appears to us as a visible embodiment of the metaphysical drive of man, which Williams has portrayed in a way far more subtle, complex and many-sided than other modern poets. Taliessin's function as a servant of both the Empire and the advent of Sarras causes his own development and significance to recede into the background. He may be a pagan, but at the same time he is *anima naturaliter christiana*, a man in quest of truth, relentless and uncompromising to the point of total self-annihilation. In addition, however, Taliessin is a poet who knows the images and the facts behind them, and who with the help of the law of correspondences senses the spiritual connections. His true home is the realm of ideas, the third heaven of the summer stars where 'unriven truths' dwell. As poet and *vates* he has known the world from the beginning and has a right to be heard, not because of his greater knowledge, but because he has literally experienced the doctrine of *largesse* and because he knows the theory of exchange, according to which each of us can and must bear the burden of others.[54]

Taliessin's followers are enslaved of their own free will: they enter the obligation on the basis of a decision of conscience and a vow, and thus their position is higher than that of the poet of the king, who has received his faith through grace.

Taliessin can preserve the image of Divine Love in his heart, even if Logres should fall. He will continue to have his following in the land, which will then be called Britain, and all those who live in love will belong to his following. And

54. On the nature and function of the poet, see William Matthew Roulet, *The Figure of the Poet in the Arthurian Poems of Charles Williams* (Diss., St John's University, 1965). The figure of the artist has a similar function in Charles Williams' novels, see Robert C. Holder, 'Art and Artist in the Fiction of Charles Williams', *Renascence*, 27 (1975), 81-7.

thus the poem of the Calling of Taliessin concludes on an almost hesitant note of resignation. Mankind 'shall follow in Logres and Britain the spiritual roads'. What binds these men together, however, and what remains after the fall of Logres, is only love, that is to say *largesse* or *caritas*.

III

The manner in which a call to the royal court or to the service of the Queen is issued is shown in *The Queen's Servant*, a difficult poem, but one of poignant beauty. Its appeal and charm lie in its conceptual terseness, its delight in magic ritual and metamorphosis. The poem sparkles with hidden energy and dynamism, and yet at the same time it relays an impression of static, almost liturgical ceremoniousness. Its beauty and charm appear to be closely akin to the baroque pomp of a high feast — they are like the scent of incense and the sound of organ music for the senses of those readers who cannot grasp the rational meaning of such intricate complexity, but who are nevertheless moved by sensual impressions, and have much the same effect as that of murmured Latin psalms, only half-understood, in a Church service.

The poem's point of departure is a letter of the seneschal Kay to Taliessin with the request to send an intelligent girl to court to serve the Queen. She must be equal to high demands: to be able to read and translate Greek, as well as to plant a rose garden, to know court ceremonial, and to understand the great art of imaginative poetry as well. The reader may be troubled in so far as he is accustomed to associating Guinevere and her sinful love with the Queen — an association which does not correspond to the intention of the poet.[55] There is still a hope of *parousia* in which the Arthurian Empire and the royal court are to play a rôle. This is the task for which the servant of the Queen is called from Taliessin's household to court. She is to provide a connection to the emperor in Byzantium, that is to the *civitas*, to serve Order on the

55. Cf. Veronica L. Skinner, 'Guinevere's role in the Arthurian poetry of Charles Williams', *Mythlore*, 4 (1977), 9-11.

spiritual plane. She is to care for it and cultivate it in the analogy of the rose garden. This double task demands a 'grand art' from her in the same manner as that possessed by the poet Taliessin. Above all it is a task which could not be entrusted to a slave. Whoever is to fulfill such an important function at court must possess the complete freedom of the Children of God. In *The Queen's Servant* we learn of the emancipation of the individual from the chains of natural concupiscence, and of the vocation and preparation for a spiritual task.

Taliessin has one of his trusted servants who is still a slave come to him, and he sets her free with a laconic word: 'Now be free'. The slave's reaction is all but enthusiastic. Rather sarcastically she answers: 'So! Freedom, I see, is the final task of servitude.' Which is as much to say, unasked for, undesired freedom is just as repressive, perhaps even more of a burden, than the service of a bondsman. One freed in this manner has to pay the ransom of her own liberation, though it is with a golden coin she has received from Taliessin. The slave knows that her liberation is not a matter of social status, but that Taliessin has signed the warrant which frees her from the entanglement of the senses and the body, thus discarding the old Adam. From this it follows that Taliessin acts as a type of Christ in these poems. The slave is commissioned to put on the new Adam, and thereby to leave behind her the barbaric status of servitude in favour of human perfection in a Christian sense and service in freedom.

Taliessin himself bought the slave in a district of Caucasia. In the anatomic myth of Williams, Caucasia means chastity and fertility of the human body, youthful freshness and the virginal unapproachability of the young girl, physical animality which forms the basis of human life; it is at the same time the location of Prometheus' martyrdom. Caucasia is therefore less a specific part of the body than the entire human body in all its naturalness: joy, energy, beauty, health, in short: the old Adam, though for the present only nature, and thus still egocentric and not yet capable of taking on the transcendental. In the organic harmony of the human limbs and their spotless beauty, Caucasia mirrors the ideal order of Byzantium as well as all that is natural. To the natives of Caucasia, however, this transcendental beauty is hidden; they do not perceive the symbolism of their country's miracles,

146

the lambs in the rose gardens, the shining snow flakes on the golden fleece of the landscape.

A prerequisite for this is an overview of the provinces of the Empire, but above all the knowledge of Byzantium and of the Imperial Palace whose throne room symbolises the omnipresence of God. All creation and therewith all themes of the realm are ultimately an expression and reflection of this central unity. The direct vision of the idea, however, is reserved for the visitor to Byzantium. Outside of the throne room there are images and symbols whose significance is only clear to those who know the idea. Only through the transcendental can the natural be understood; only intellect knows that it knows.

The slave has never been in Byzantium and will probably never reach it. But she is capable of grasping the referential character of her body intellectually — through the study of metaphysical books or through Merlin's maps, or even through the mysterious little book from the library of the emperor. But there is an easier and quicker approach: man becomes capable of receiving the transcendental when he puts off the old Adam. 'Unclothe' is the command which Taliessin gives to the slave, and therewith she stands before him in the immaculate beauty of her shining nakedness. Taliessin gazes at the organic unity of beauteous soul in beauteous body, and in it he sees a premonition of the prayer of the nun Dindrane and the benediction of Galahad.

As in *The Calling of Taliessin*, the body of the woman is transformed under the meditative stare of Taliessin into the world. A few hints lead us to conclude that Taliessin's eyes rest on the back of the maiden, and that this in turn becomes identical with the shadow of Caucasia, in which the tiny but clearly visible shadow of Byzantium blossoms, and even the meadows of Sarras beyond the sea. This second metamorphosis of the human back excludes the possibility of a coincidental play on images, and this applies to *The Calling of Taliessin* as well. In my opinion, this is Williams' central metaphor. The human body is in itself a microcosm, which is simultaneously a reflection of the greater world and a world in itself. The term alone implies the existence of a macrocosm with similar features and qualities. Williams expresses the universe in terms of the image of the human body, which not only serves as a major symbol of the poet's concept of

147

life and the world, but also as the focus of his poetic vision.

The origin of the image is possibly to be seen in Exodus XXXIII. 23 which states that Moses may only see the back of God: '. . . and [I] will cover thee with my hand until I have passed by: and I will take away mine hand, and thou shalt see my back: but my face shall not be seen'. The back of God is usually interpreted as the material world. Thus Moses experiences in his vision the entirety of the world in an image similar to that seen by his successor Taliessin who reveals parallels to his great predecessor in more than this point. But even the Bible is not alone in this image. We find similar forms in many myths of creation, for instance in the Nordic Song of Ymir, according to which the sea was made from the blood of the arch-giant Ymir, the mountains from his bones, the land from his flesh, the stones from his teeth and the trees from his hair.

The most striking parallel to Williams is to be found in Blake whose giant Albion contained everything in himself before his fall: sun, moon, stars, and sea.[56] Only the imagination is capable of uniting the interior with the exterior in a manner which may even approach the mystical, so that in human society we catch a glimpse of the true presence of the divine body of Christ.[57]

Williams is also concerned with the relation of nature and the transcendental, but they do not represent separate units

56. According to Blake, the main characteristic of John Locke's philosophy is the externalisation of the existence of material objects.

57. Cf. Northrop Frye, *Fearful Symmetry. A Study of William Blake* (Boston, 3rd ed., 1967), 349 ff. A comparison of the stars in heaven with the body of Christ is to be found in Richard Rolle. It is an interesting fact that he writes: 'Also, swet Jhesu, þe sterres ben cause of euche þynge þat is grene, or groweth, or bereth fruyt . . . Also sterris ben cause of mynys, metaill, and of precious stonys . . .' *English Writings of Richard Rolle*, ed. H. E. Allen (Oxford, 1963), 35. The Metaphysical poets often compare the human body to the universe (e.g. George Herbert, in 'Man'), as does mystical poetry in general. Cf. John Charles Earle, 'Bodily Extension': '. . . Thus every man / Wears as his robe the garment of the sky − / So close his union with the cosmic plan, / So perfectly he pierces low and high − / Reaching as far in space as creature can, / And coextending with immensity.' *Oxford Book of English Mystical Verse* (Oxford, 1962), 510.

for him; they are intermingled. Caucasia has cast its shadow on Sarras, and thus rendered it visible like an image or a metaphor which contains its object of reference in a figurative sense in itself. Only when the body of the slave is naked and humbled, is it prepared for the glorious robe of an all-encompassing reality which is given to man with his freedom. In place of her old garb, the girl is given a robe of roses and wool. Only the old girdle is to be retained as a reminder of her former servitude, and as a warning to remain true to her new obligation.[58]

The central image of the poem is the exchange of clothes. It derives from Paul's *Epistle to the Corinthians*, V.4ff.: 'For verily in this we groan, longing to be clothed upon with our habitation which is from heaven: if so be that being clothed we shall not be found naked. For indeed we that are in this tabernacle do groan, being burdened; not for that we would be unclothed, but that we would be clothed upon, that what is mortal may be swallowed up of life . . . Wherefore if any man is in Christ, he is a new creature: the old things are passed away; behold, they are become new.' The apostle compares man's earthly body with a temporary tent, the heavenly body with a permanent house. But he wishes to put on the heavenly body in this life, without having to first cross the threshold of death.

The exchange of clothes in Charles Williams can only be understood in the context of the *Epistle to the Corinthians*. It stands for a spiritual metamorphosis, the transition from the status of natural corporality to a new life in the spirit. The poetic metaphor which symbolises this is the cloak of golden lambs' wool and red roses; nor are these just any roses, but rather Caucasian centifoliae. The characteristic of this species is their scarlet colour and the heart-shaped centre of their petals. This is a good example of the way Charles Williams uses metaphors: they glow from within with rich sensuality and yet at the same time they are transformed into an abstract concept which can only be derived from the original image through abstraction and thoughtful reflection. It is much the same as the manner in which the poet Taliessin

58. Gawain's reason for wearing the green girdle was a similar one. In general, this item of clothing appears to have borne a corresponding function in courtly poetry.

plucks the string of his harp and immediately grasps it with two fingers to prevent it from resonating further. The scarlet colour of the rose and the shape of the heart, the wool of the symbolic animal, the lamb, all signal the meaning of the clothes and at the same time the metamorphosis of the slave.

The way to sanctification leads through nature, that is through the works of Nimue, who continually shapes the things of this world according to their archetypes in the third heaven. The transformation requires the 'rhythms of ceremony', the 'grand art', but also grace. By grand art Williams apparently means a sacramental, liturgical art, and by grace the divine power from which art stems. Both are necessary for the sanctification of flesh and blood.

The liberation of the slave ends with an act of exchange, *largesse*. Taliessin imbues her with his entire power and energy, and there is a genuine exchange of qualities and features. Williams believed quite literally in the possibility of such a substitution. He not only rediscovered the doctrine of the Atonement and reinterpreted it back into art and experience; he was also convinced that each of us could take upon himself the burden of another, and, in turn, share his energy and power with his neighbour.[59] 'Substitutionary love transcends the "fallacy of rational virtue" which says we are judged by our own works – *only*.'[60] The power of Taliessin pours into the slave in a blast of union. This blast means both a union of nature and spirit, as well as the descent of the Spirit, the experience of the Divine. Through this the slave has become an equal of Taliessin, she henceforth belongs to Taliessin's Society. 'Be as Ourself in Logres.' This command is valid to death, even beyond death, for afterwards there can be no fear of death but only yearning for the beyond, as we read in St Paul.

The ceremonial conclusion of the act of liberation is thus to be seen as a kind of confirmation (*confirmatio*) which finds expression in the blow to the cheek. This detail originates from the Roman ceremony of the freeing of

59. On the problem of 'exchange' and Williams' doctrine of substitution and its psychological and existential foundation, see J. J. Boies, 'Existential Exchange in the Novels of Charles Williams', *Renascence*, 26 (1974), 219-229.

60. Martin J. Moynihan, in a private communication to the author.

prisoners, but here it carries the additional sense of making one strong for the battle of life, but last not least also the kind of salvation 'after the kind of Christ and the order of Logres'. The central idea of the poem is God:

'Depart, with God,' She said: 'Remain, in God.'

IV

The girl from Caucasia is called to the royal court. Although she is liberated and belongs to Taliessin's following, she is still a child in a spiritual sense and thus in constant danger of a relapse. With *The Coming of Galahad*, however, the new Adam comes to Arthur's court. Mysterious things happen which cause everyone to recognise that the prophecies of the arrival of the Chosen One are about to be fulfilled: Galahad takes his seat at the Round Table, the famous *Siège Périlleux*, without being swallowed up by the earth, as his unworthy predecessors had been. The knights receive from the Grail everything they wish in the way of food and drink, and the water Galahad washes his hands with glitters and sparkles like a thousand stars. At the close of the evening the knight of the Grail is led to Arthur's bed in a ceremonial procession. He takes possession of it after a mysterious rite: the New Adam takes the place of the Old.[61]

We view all this with Taliessin as outsiders from the perspective of servants and kitchen-boys. The king's poet has not joined the procession. He passes through offices and kitchens to the exterior courtyard, from where he views the torch-lit procession to the king's bed seen through the windows of towers and halls: 'He stood looking up among the jakes and latrines', and even the nursery rhyme which he sings to his own accompaniment on the harp contains the descending motion which we have just passed through with the poet:

Down the porphyry stair the queen's child ran,
There he played with his father's crown . . .

61. Cf. Charles Moorman, *Arthurian Triptych*, 72.

We have already reached the lowest point of descent, for we stand in the outer courtyard before the latrines and therewith at the outer point of Williams' organic and physiological symbolism. This is where the discussion between Taliessin, Gareth and a slave takes place, and its topic is 'preference', the hierarchy of Logres and the significance of Galahad, the keeper of the Grail: 'Lord, tell me of the new knight!' 'What man is this for whom the emperor lifts the Great Ban?' For Williams the answer to this question was particularly important, since it was decisive for the values and meanings of his own philosophy of life. Religion, philosophy, poetry, love: each of these represented a closed, autonomous world for him, one which resisted integration into an overall structure.

Taliessin sings the Song of Songs for Galahad. He has no doubt that this knight stands at the top of the world hierarchy and that he is justified in taking his place in Arthur's bed. But Taliessin sings among the jakes and latrines, he stands at the other end of the scale, among human excrement which reminds him and others of the fact that the flight to the mysterious heights of the Grail must start from the basis of human nature, and that all paths to the realm must lead through the door of man's animality. I would see the jakes as a first hint of man's feet of clay — his weakness and proneness to error, and thus a premonition of the eventual failure of a union of Camelot and Carbonek.

The poem of *The Coming of Galahad* is dominated by the symbolism of stone and shell which Williams has taken from Wordsworth's *Prelude*. The fifth book of this work begins with a dream of the poet. In the midst of a desert, a mounted Bedouin appears bearing a stone in one hand, in the other a shell of exquisite beauty. The stone stands for the doctrine of Euclid, geomety, and the shell for poetical song, poetry. The stone and shell become the poles of Williams' thought, and symbolise for him order and life, Byzantium and Broceliande, Nimue and the third heaven. Stone and shell are fused, and become one in the person of Galahad. He is the image of the new Adam and an example of the necessary union of the realms of Arthur and the Grail in Logres.

Taliessin believes that he has seen the union in five different houses: in poetry; in the life of the senses and of the body; in the intellect; in religion; and in the imaginative vision (Byzantium), and even in double form in each house. Intellectual Gaul requires the shell in order to reach perfection; corporeal Caucasia requires the stone. All the houses are intimately connected with each other, each is autonomous, but requires the other to give and receive validity and permanence. It seems to me that Taliessin speaks a clear and understandable language at this point. He sees the five houses transformed into the triangle of the pentagram which before had played such a great rôle in Merlin's magic as a symbol of perfection.

The direct source of Williams and thus the key to a better understanding of his imagery may well be seen in the Middle English romance *Sir Gawain and the Green Knight*, in which Gawain carries the pentagram as a heraldic symbol on his shield. The allegorical meaning of this symbol rests in the idea of the 'endless knot', so named because the star is composed of an unbroken connection of five lines which, when traced, lead right back to the point of departure. Taliessin traces the lines of the pentagram with his finger, and the individual significance of the houses is lost from sight. One dissolves into another. Taliessin's skill fails him, for it is only adequate for the single categories. In the pentagram, however, they are submerged in a single identity.

The recognition of identity is made possible by the fusion of shell and stone, the creation of a new quality. Logres likewise can only gain its identity from a similar synthesis. At first, the dual character of truly fulfilled existence is to be observed in each individual house. Lewis describes the first and foremost taks of life as: 'to "fit" the stone and the shell in whatever House you occupy, to retain poetic vision in the midst of hard thinking, to study "precision" in your highest poetry, to offer even to the *body* of the beloved a "Euclidean love" '.[62]

But the balance achieved in this way is only valid in the individual house, and this is not the end of the task. The category province remains an organic part of the Empire, that is to say of the higher order. True identity can only be achieved by a fusion of the categories with one another: 'The clerks of the Emperor's house study the redaction of categories into identity: so we'.[63] In the person of Galahad, a

62. *Arthurian Torso*, 168.
63. 'The Coming of Galahad', in *Taliessin Through Logres*, 69-77, here 73.

shoot of the third heaven has taken root in Logres; the symbol of the pentagram is tailored to fit him. It stands for the fusion of cateogries to a single identity and therewith transcends Taliessin's comprehension: 'What then . . . when the cut hazel has nothing to measure?'[64] The poet is forced to retreat, modest and humble. A new measure must be applied in the future:

> . . . The eyes of my lord are the measure of intensity
> and his arms of action; the hazel, Blanchefleur, he.[65]

The Coming of Galahad concludes with Taliessin's vision of the ascent of the soul to the innermost heaven. Similar to Dante who had seen the planetary spheres in analogy to the different grades of holiness, Williams draws an analogy between the planets and their zones and the spiritual and mental development of man. Four zones divide the Empire from the throne of God and are to be passed through in the development of man and therewith of the City. In the face of a geocentric structure of the universe in *The Calling of Taliessin*, this centripetal movement appears contradictory and illogical.[66] But we must recall that according to Dante and to other medieval authorities spatial order mirrors the spiritual one. According to this view, the earth is located at the outermost fringe of the universe, that is to say before the walls of the City. Man was once the centre of the universe and now stands on its fringes.

The last part of the poem is difficult because the basic concept of the interior part of the courtyard of the palace is meant to stand as a kind of base for the planetarium. Williams says that four zones separate the Empire from the throne of God, and these zones are 'slanted to each cleft in each wall, with planets planted.' In this we hear an echo of the beginning of the poem: 'till he came by a door cleft in a smooth wall'. Thus Taliessin stands in the interior courtyard and views the spheres of the planets slanted towards the sight-holes in the wall, on the one side Mercury and Venus, on the other Jupiter and Saturn. He himself stands upon the Earth,

64. 'The Coming of Galahad', 72.

65. 'The Coming of Galahad', 73.

66. Cf. C. S. Lewis, *The Discarded Image*, 58.

'seen and strewn by the four'. To the careful reader, this passage reveals a correction of the medieval planetarium: Mercury and Venus circulate beneath the Earth around the sun, Jupiter and Saturn are planets with larger orbits. It is possible that Williams superimposed this modern view of the planetary system intentionally upon the original model, not to mystify the reader, but in order to demonstrate that the poetic mode is not tied to the 'Discarded Image', but is an appropriate and valid vehicle of the twentieth century and its view of the world. The basis of the poem at any rate is a geocentrical view of the universe. Earth is symbolised by the courtyard, on which the spheres of the individual planets are slanted like the props of a baldachin which rise up to the firmament and direct the meditative gaze of the *Vates* towards the throne of God.

The first step of the ascent is marked by the planet Mercury; it corresponds to the God of Conflict and Change, the as yet undecided state of rivalry among the houses. Venus represents the sphere of the focussing of human thought on a certain goal ('Venus preference'), an interior turning towards a loved one. Jupiter with its moons indicates irony and irony vanquished, which no longer bruises itself on the unavoidable, but accepts the wonderful absurdity of it all and laughs about it. And finally Saturn is the star of loneliness and meditation,[67] of the promise and image of Golden Age.[68] Logres, as Taliessin sees, has only reached the sphere of Jupiter. Here Galahad and Lancelot still live with one another, unrest of the heart and earthliness. Future developments are already anticipated: the huge powers of Broceliande have created Galahad but have exhausted themselves in the act. Logres bows down to Britannia; Carbonek and Camelot are by no means one, but are farther apart than ever before.

---

67. *The Divine Comedy of Dante Alighieri*, Paradiso, Canto XXI, 532-537.

68. Cf. Ferdinand Piper, *Mythologie der christlichen Kunst von der ältesten Zeit bis in's* [sic] *sechzehnte Jahrhundert* (Weimar, 1851), 215.

The poem *The Meditation of Mordred* is far clearer and simpler than the preceding ones. We hear no more of mystic Sarras and of the perfection of man on earth. The subject is now Logres, which is to develop into historical Britain. The aureole of the transcendental gradually recedes, giving way to the naked reality of things which are only reflections and which have lost their tie with the third heaven. Mordred himself is a totally down-to-earth type, one no longer ambivalent but completely autonomous, evil, perverted, and cynical. He is the incestuous son of Arthur, and thus the symbol of destructive egotism which Williams calls Gomorrha.

The reader is not led to judge Mordred on the basis of his deeds, but rather on his state of inner consciousness. The entire poem consists of an interior monologue which makes a brutally open description of the happenings in Logres possible. Mordred is not subject to any restrictions or inhibitions. His thoughts are disjointed and only connected by association. The single law of his psychology is a perverted yearning for recognition, aimed at a paradise in the style of the cruel dictators of the Antipodes.

The names and events are taken from Malory's *Morte Darthur*, which is to be seen as a background for the entire cycle. The date of the events can be fixed through the name of Pope Deodatus, who succeeded Boniface IV and was head of the church from 615 to 618. The introduction of this historical personage into the world of cryptic mythology can be seen as a confirmation of the tendency towards reality. The clouds of phantasy begin to recede, the transcendentally beautiful figures of a long-awaited, imaginatively anticipated *parousia* disappear like swirls of mist before the noon-day sun. The world shows her true face.

The first lines of the poem contain a play on the various meanings of *wood* and *elm*. Usually, the elm is connected with pleasurable associations in poetry. It represents the human qualities of beauty, charm, graciousness and stateliness.[69] But Arthur has all the elms of his country torne down to make poles and oars, to carry his knights across the

69. Gertraud Jobes, ed., *Dictionary of Mythology, Folklore and Symbols* (New York, 1961).

Channel: 'The king has poled his horsemen across the Channel.' And once they are on the other side of the Channel, the poles of elm become human-like beings which stand motionless about Lancelot's castle.

In Mordred's eyes, the reason for this campaign is miserable, unworthy and banal. In Malory's *Morte Darthur*, the underlying law of war was determined by the tragic inevitability of a world approaching its downfall, one which sucked Arthur into its vortex. According to Williams' Mordred, the only reason for the siege is: 'lest . . . the king should be cheated with another by his wife the queen.' Disinterested and completely detached, the traitor sees, in his imagination, the besieging troops from the roof of the palace. In his vivid fantasy the knights of King Arthur are transformed into spears of elmwood. But these elms break into bud, 'the elms bud in steel points', and these are directed against the walls of Benwick, behind which Lancelot rests secure and safe from danger.

From Arthur and Lancelot, the traitor's thoughts turn to Guinevere who has evidently hidden herself in the Convent of Almesbury out of fear and disdain for Mordred. According to a number of other versions, Guinevere plots with Mordred, thereby sinking to his moral level. Williams sees her in the image of 'stone fitting itself to its echo',[70] entangled in her own circle of life like sound and echo, infertile and pale, basically unworthy of her great lover Lancelot. In Mordred's eyes, Guinevere is a whore, and Arthur correspondingly an old cuckold. In this respect his cynicism is unparalleled: 'It is laidly alike to be a wittol and a whore.'[71]

Mordred's opinion of the inhabitants of London is no higher. In his eyes they are capable of stoning Guinevere in a sudden attack of fanatic righteousness, should he decide to drag the Queen out of the Convent by force and lead her

70. 'The Coming of Galahad', 74.

71. 'The Meditation of Mordred', in *The Region of the Summer Stars*, 47-9, here 47. The word 'laidly' presents difficulties in the interpretation. In my opinion, it is to be seen both as a pun on 'ladylike' and on the verb 'to lay', to which it could be considered an adverb; the passage clearly contains a sexual innuendo, and the Scottish 'laidly' in the sense of 'repulsive', 'hideous', 'offensive', appears a less likely probability. 'Wittol' is an old word for cuckold.

through the streets of London. This is evidently a thought with which Mordred has played for a long time – a result of his disappointment in Guinevere. All Londoners are self-righteous and have thus forfeited the grace of coinherence. Catholic morals and catholic mockery are counterpoised. Catholic, in the first word-pair, is capitalized and means Catholic in the ecclesiastical sense. In contrast, the 'catholic' paired with mockery is not capitalized and carries the meaning 'universal', widespread. But this play on the meaning of words is more than a simple pun, for the term catholic mockery designates at the same time the degeneration of catholic morality to a self-righteous, loveless condemnation of the sins of one's neighbour: exchange and *largesse* are dead in the land, London has regressed from the City to the wood: 'London is become a forest . . . bare grinning leaves, a whole wood of moral wantons, whose spines are tree-stretched up towards me, their hope.' For Williams the forest represents the primeval and the wild, as yet unformed chaos, lacking definition and horizon.[72] The principle of order has been lost. Camelot is no longer the head of the realm which is to see the birth of the new Adam. It has made itself independent, in rebellion against its Byzantine centre.

The unity symbolized by an organic body has been destroyed. The old tribute is abolished. The gold coins with the sign of the dragon will remain in the country: London has declared its autonomy. But the symbol of the dragon is not only found on the coins; it is also Mordred's coat of arms, so that he is entitled to say: 'Kin to kin presently, children; I too am a dragon.' Like many other symbols in the poem, the dragon which was once the heraldic cognizance of Uther and Arthur has taken on an ominous connotation and appearance, and thus carries a different meaning to that in previous treatments of the Arthurian material.[73] With right, Taliessin says in a previous conversation with Kay:

Sir, if you made verse you would doubt symbols.
I am afraid of the little loosed dragons.
When the means are autonomous, they are deadly; . . .[74]

72. *The Image of the City*, 'Introduction', lii.

73. Cf. the author's treatment in 'Die Wappen König Arthurs in der Hs. Lansdowne 882', *Anglia*, 79 (1961), 253-266, here 253.

74. 'Bors to Elayne: On the King's Coins', in *Taliessin Through Logres*, 42-5, here 44.

The loosed dragons which are directed against their own country remind the reader of the *Alliterative Morte Arthure*[75] in which Arthur dreams of a dragon which will one day destroy his land. The philosophers and interpreters of the dream assure the king that he himself is symblized by the dragon. His own *hubris* will cause the downfall of his realm. But also his son Mordred (Welsh *mordraig* = sea dragon) plays an important part in this. In Charles Williams, this same Mordred is practically the incarnation of the sinful egotism of his father. Thus we should not reproach the son when he says: 'Like son, like father'.

Mordred regards the holy vessel of the Grail in a very similar way. Even here, we see an all-pervading degeneration of values. In *The Calling of Taliessin* Ceridwen's cauldron was a typological anticipation of the Grail. But Mordred does not believe in such a Grail. He recalls that his father often pondered the importance of this holy vessel for his salvation. But he will and can do without such a fairy mechanism. If there were something like the Grail, he says, he would have it carried off by a dozen knights. His cooks would be pleased to possess such a magic cauldron.

The Grail seen as a cooking pot in Mordred's kitchen — this represents the absolute depth of degradation of the mystical and the sacred. All associations with the Eucharist and the creation of a new Adam have been abandoned. For Mordred the Grail is no more than a magic device to be handled with care, because a fairy might be summoned to the room at a rubbing as with Aladdin's lamp.

The idea of Aladdin's lamp leads Mordred's thoughts to exotic climes. All the themes and provinces of the Byzantine Empire have been destroyed, for they have lost their coherence. And now Mordred dreams of a kingdom of his own, a kind of Anti-Empire, 'beyond miles of bamboo' (12.1), one which has a number of similarities to P'o-l'u, which lies even beyond this terrible country: 'beyond P'o-l'u / he told of another Empire . . . where a small Emperor sits' (13.2-4). This emperor becomes a model for Mordred, who is evidently impressed most by his relationship to his small, slant-eyed wives: once or twice every seven years he has one brought into his bed or thrown into a swamp in a bamboo cage. This

75. Ed. Krishna (New York, 1976).

159

is the type of tyrant Mordred wants to be. He intends to establish an Empire in London, as soon as his father is fallen in the wood of elms. His paradise is to be like that of the tyrant of the Antipodes, and he wants to live there by himself and to be admired by all other men.

Mordred is not Satan; he is probably not even the incarnation of evil. Williams sees him as a man of flesh and blood, the product of criminal incest and the expression of Arthur's egotistic love of self: 'her arm was stretched to embrace his own stretched arm; she had his own face'.[76] Thus Mordred is exclusively self-directed in all his thoughts and intentions. He rejects the attempt at integration into a larger society and draws his standard of value for his action solely from his own impulses. '. . . Mordred is entire egotism, Arthur's self-attention carried to the final degree. This is why it is he who wrecks the Table.'[77]

The difference between father and son rests in the fact that Arthur desires the good but is too weak to achieve it, in spite of others and himself. Mordred, however, embodies the diabolic aspect of the dragon. Of course, he is also an exemplary embodiment of original sin and man's need for salvation. But in addition he is an individual, and as such he has freedom of choice and can decide for himself. There were a number of other possibilities open to him — Charles Williams has shown them clearly enough. But Mordred's decision is a selfish one — against *largesse*, exchange and coherence. And thus it appears to me that we have more than just the archetype of evil in a mythological poem and more than a fascinating, clearly visualized figure in a lyric cycle. Here we have the prototype of modern man, who is incapable of loving his neighbour unless he needs him for his own purposes, who takes the salvation of the soul into his own hands and prunes morality as the situation demands, who holds the spiritual world for no more than fairy magic and superstition.

We recognise him: he is the autonomous man cut off from all attachments; he is the succubus in love with his own image, the narcissist who transforms coinherence into in-

---

76. 'Lamorack and the Queen Morgause of Orkney', in *Taliessin Through Logres*, 38-41, here 40.

77. *The Image of the City*, 176.

coherence and will nevertheless be respected, admired and honoured. Not until the concluding poem, *The Prayers of the Pope*, does it become clear where these developments lead.

VI

The Prayers of the Pope represents a turbulent, eventful crescendo of historical events and developments which lead to the final catastrophe — the downfall of the realm and the dissolution of Taliessin's fellowship. The event is not described in an epic way by the poet, but rather as the reflection of the young Pope Deodatus, as he prepares himself for the Eucharistic service of Christmas by a meditation in the Lateran Church: 'slender, white-haired, incandescent, seeming in his trance of prayer a third twin of Merlin and Brisen, . . .'[78] The white hair of the young man is a sign of premature aging under the burden of an office of great responsibility. We know that the historical Deodatus II once invested his entire strength in the attempt to bring Rome and Byzantium together. But for Williams the symbol of white hair means a great deal more: 'And do you think the Pope, who is young, with white hair, brilliant, the image of Merlin (only M[erlin] has black hair), might be Merlin + [sic] loss? If you get me. The Pope (let us say) is time losing its beauties (by deprivation or will, not by mere passing change) but affirmatively. O I write it badly . . .'[79]

As welcome and interesting this foot-note of Williams may be, it does not seem to me as necessary for the understanding of the poem as Anne Ridler maintains: 'I could not see how any reader would be able to guess the significance of the Pope's white hair or understand why he is said to be *rich* in loss without such a hint.'[80] My own impression is that the poet is meditating upon his own poem, and that the results of his reflection are just as unique and unusual as his use of metaphor and symbolism in the poem. The only prerequisite

78. 'Prayers of the Pope', in *The Regions of the Summer Stars*, 50-61, here 50.

79. *The Image of the City*, Introduction, lxv.

80. *The Image of the City*, Introduction, lxv.

161

actually necessary for an understanding of the poem is the basic structure of the Byzantine Empire, and even that could be interpolated from a close reading of the poems themselves.

The individual images, concepts and thoughts behind the poem gain a general imaginative relevance through a continual transposition of levels and perspectives. They are not restricted to a single case or historical fact, as for instance the invasion of the Huns, the break between Papacy and Patriarchy (1054), the World War; rather they represent a kind of law of history in a metaphorical manner. Every Logres has become Britannia in the course of its historical development. Grail, Christ and the Eucharist are manifested on earth, but men do not live on earth untouched by history. The call goes unheeded, the image recedes and is lost for ever. There is no consolation in the fact that after all it is only an image that has been lost, that is to say something transitory and unstable. Williams objects:

> But each loss of each image
> is single and full, a thing unrequited,
> plighted in presence to no recompense, . . .[81]

To live in and with images belongs to the nature of man, who is met half-way by God in that he relinquished his own essence and became man.[82] Therewith God reaffirms the justification of the images through and in himself. Thus the Pope prays: '. . . confirm / nor thee in thine images only but thine images in thee.'[83]

With particular clarity and audibility, connotations of the last World War are felt. Williams, with his poet's sensibility, experienced and suffered its ordeal to a degree hardly rivalled by another Englishman. In London and Paris, the poet says, the peace talks were silenced, the cities of Logres 'felt the sliding planes of the raiders' sails'. Very gradually this vision of the Second World War is replaced by images of the

81. 'Prayers of the Pope', 50.

82. On the Neoplatonic character of Williams' imagery, and his theological basis in Thomas Aquinas' *analogia entis*, see Sape Anne Zylstra, *Charles Williams: An Analysis and Appraisal of his Major Work* (Diss., Emory University, 1969).

83. 'Prayers of the Pope', 55.

invasion of the Huns, who cross the Weichsel, Danube and Rhine and flood Europe: 'the land shook / as band after band stamped into darkness cities / whose burning had lamped their path.' Finally these cruel images of war are matched by implications of the Japanese invasion of India, a case of uncanny foresight, since this part of the poem was first written before the war.[84] At the same time, however, it is also strongly reminiscent of the octopus-like menace described in Wells' *War of the Worlds*. But perhaps one should not interpret the image of the octopi who creep from coast to coast with their giant tentacles, 'feeling along Burma, nearing India' too concretely. The basic conception is the extension of the headless Emperor's power and that of his realm (P'o-l'u) through the destruction of the Empire.

Hardly a word is wasted at this point on the realm of Arthur and the knights of the Round Table. We learn of the complex events which lead to downfall, not through the poet's direct account, but through rumours which reach the ears of the Pope via various indirect channels. At first we hear only of Arthur's war against Lancelot, of Gawain's irreconcilability and his preference for private vengeance, but most of all of Mordred, the incarnation of treachery and discord. The letters of the Pope have achieved nothing at all, the disease of chaos has spread in the whole country, and mobs storm through the streets of London – a symbol for interior rebellion, the dissolution of the City. Mordred takes possession of the Round Table and fills it with pagan chieftains. With the demon of his own desire, he fashions a world of false images without any mutual relationship or coherence: 'Logres was void of Grail and Crown.'

From Taliessin's mouth we hear the account of the end of Arthur's realm. In terse words the poet and seer informs his followers that Arthur and all the lords of the Round Table are dead: 'the Table may end to-morrow'. This example makes it particularly evident that Williams' intention differs from that of Malory. The core of the matter is no longer the ascent and the downfall of the realm of Arthur, but the destruction of the Empire, that is of order and unity, of organic coherence and *largesse* among men, of the ceasing of exchange, and the loss of coinherence.

84. *Arthurian Torso*, 185.

And thus it is the downfall of the kingdom that forms the subject of the poem. The inhabitants live in a constant state of fear of others; they become isolated and strive for complete autonomy and self-justification. They exist solely in the aura of their own glory, and as a necessary consequence, view their fellow man as a natural enemy. This is true of groups, as well as of individuals. Those who reject the society of the city and would place the nation, race, or people in its stead require a counterbalance against which they can clarify and consolidate their own goals. Nationalism, racism and class conflict all entail enmity against someone — foreigners, Jews or capitalists:[85] 'forsaking the Emperor, they chose among themselves, / here one and there one, foes / among themselves, puppets of reputation, / void of communicated generation of glory.'[86]

Even the form in which the message of the poem is couched is indicative of the collapse of order and coherence. Interjected parenthetical remarks break sentence periods into small groups, independent both in rhythm and content and loosely joined by apposition. The resultant impression is one of incoherence and dissolution. The identity of the kingdom as an organic whole dissolves, the categories become autonomous, and there is no longer a Merlin to unite them in the pentagram. At the same time, the disintegration of the provinces also means the dissolution of the organic body — that is to say, death: 'all gave their choice to the primal curse and the grave, . . .'[87] Each is prepared to consign his neighbour to eternal damnation; each becomes a Mordred, or a Khan of the Huns, or the Calif of Asia in his heart. The city gives way to autonomous sects, and the poets are replaced by men who either cannot speak at all, or are only capable of spouting empty rhetoric. Magicians conjure up the ghosts of the past, which rise from Hell and from their graves to form a macabre procession — an army of mindless bodies in mechanical motion at the fore of the pagan hordes. This part of the poem, with its terrible visions, reveals the depth of

85. Cf. *Arthurian Torso*, 182.

86. 'The Prayers of the Pope', 51.

87. 'The Prayers of the Pope', 51.

Williams' 'knowledge of darkness',[88] his painful, nightmare-like certainty of the true existence of evil as the result of original sin.

But for Williams there are no clear-cut lines between Good and Evil. He refuses to join in the biased, one-sided condemnation of the enemy and the self-justification of 'Our Side' and its motivation. 'Where is the difference between us?' asks the Pope. 'Causes and catapults they have and we have.' He refuses to sit in judgment, 'alive are they in us and we in them. / We know how we have sinned; we know not how they.'[89] The only difference lies in the fact that the Pope's side acknowledges *coinherence*, whereas the other side denies it. Herein lies the true task of the Church in Williams' eyes: to realize its Catholicity and its universality. In all things Williams preferred the whole to the parts; he rejected the Roman Catholic Church for denying true Catholicism when it proclaimed itself the sole guardian of Christian truth, thereby creating a schism with the universal church. But this did not mean that he rejected Rome or the Papacy. For Williams, Byzantium, Canterbury, Jerusalem and Rome represented provinces of a single Christian church.[90]

Williams has Pope Deodatus sense the schism in his own heart, the collapse of order and the return of chaos. All the prayers of the Pope close with the same repeated lines, which echo like a refrain: 'Send not, send not the rich empty away!' Pope Deodatus feels the disintegration and spiritual death in his soul – the downward progress of the Kingdom has reached its lowest point. Charles Williams leaves us in a world similar to that of T. S. Eliot's *Waste Land*, where the Fisher-King's question is answered by a nursery rhyme: 'London Bridge is falling down, falling down, falling down . . .' There is no reprieve from the curse of sterility.

But Williams also leaves us a small gleam of hope: Taliessin's household will survive. Although the poet relinquishes his task to God and formally dissolves the existing bonds, the ideal society will live on, and all will belong who

88. Cf. the chapter of the same name in A. M. Hadfield, *An Introduction to Charles Williams* (London, 1959).

89. 'The Prayers of the Pope', 53.

90. Cf. Hadfield, *Introduction*, 131.

165

are united by love. Secretly, unbeknownst to each other, and completely on their own, men will continue to love their neighbour and to serve their fellow man. They will continue to do good, for good in this world can no more be stamped out than can evil.

And Taliessin gives the reader a further hope: Broceliande will live forever. Even though the tentacles of P'o-l'u approach the coast of India, they encounter resistance: they are held fast and prevented from further progress by something similar to them and yet completely alien — the roots of the magic forest of Broceliande. They twine themselves firmly about the powerful arms of P'o-l'u; the powers of death and the Underworld are held in check by the Mother of Making.

Thus hope for mankind lies in the fact that evil can never gain total ascendancy. Broceliande and P'o-l'u merge, and there is continual encounter between the outgrowth of Evil and the seedling-like growth of Good, which may at times be forced to retreat, but can never be fully overcome. This is the hope which lives on in mankind and inspires the lords and consuls whose hearts preserve the dream of the Empire and who continue to hope for the advent of Sarras in spite of all darkness and despair.

VII

The question which must be raised in conclusion is whether or not Charles Williams can be regarded as a modern poet. Where are we to place him, and what position does his thought represent? The *avant garde* of today would hardly accept him as one of their own, for their categorical demand on 'modern poetry' is that it translate the individual view of life from the plane of purely personal emotion, experience, and knowledge to the open and unlimited reaches of potential experience. Modern lyric poetry is expected to be negative, rejecting idealistic concepts of life in favour of the open-endedness of human existence. According to this school, modern lyric poetry tends to veil its subject in enigma and intentional ambiguity, rather than to reveal it in the light of the easily understood. Thus images are reduced to abstract stimuli divorced from reality, meant to cancel out still other images in the dynamics of dialectical motion. Charles Williams can hardly be called 'modern' in this sense. On the other hand, a number of his qualities have gained the approval of the strictly *avant garde* — his effective use of hyperbole and over-kill, of enigma and evocation, of the cipher and the shock of 'revelation'.[91]

The fact that Charles Williams edited the poems of Gerard Manley Hopkins tells us a great deal.[92] The poems were first published by Bridges in 1918, and they left a deep impression on Williams as a young man: 'The poems were a literary sensation. All the papers reviewed them; everyone who was anyone talked of them.'[93] And yet it was not until 1929 (eleven years after the first appearance of the poems in an edition of 750 copies) that a new edition was called for. Bridges was occupied with work on his *Testament of Beauty* and thus entrusted Williams with the task. After extensive research, the young poet wrote an introduction to the second edition and added further unpublished poems of Hopkins' in an appendix.

Like many of his contemporaries, Williams read the poems of this unvictorian Victorian with admiration, but without losing his critical detachment: 'We could even smile while we admired.'[94] Williams must suddenly have realized that certain of the techniques used by Hopkins were better suited for his own needs than the complex verse forms and somewhat colourless blank verse used until that time.[95]

Above all, Hopkins' device of 'sprung rhythm' was to

91. Gustav René Hocke, *Manierismus in der Literatur* (Hamburg, 1961), 301; on the following see: *Poems of G. M. Hopkins*, ed. A. W. Gardner (London, 3rd edn. 1949); D. Morris, *The Poetry of G. M. Hopkins and T. S. Eliot in the Light of the Donne Tradition* (Diss., Bern, 1951); R. Haas, *Wege zur englischen Lyrik* (Heidelberg, 1962), 135-8.

92. Concerning the influence of Gerard Manley Hopkins on Williams' 'new style', see Vernon-Leland Ingraham, *The Verse Drama of Charles Williams* (Diss., University of Pennsylvania, 1965).

93. 'Gerard Hopkins. Time and Tide review of Dr Gardner's study, 1945', in *The Image of the City*, 48-51, here 49.

94. 'Gerard Hopkins. Time and Tide review . . .', 48.

95. On the following, cf. *The Image of the City*, 'Introduction', lxiff.

prove fruitful and inspiring for the *Arthuriad*. Williams has made various comments on the fact that this metre originally derived from Germanic alliterative poetry, rather than being invented by Hopkins. Even if this view were justified, Hopkins must be given credit for having re-discovered the technique of stressed alliterative verse and rendering it a suitable medium for expressing the essence of things in a form (*in-shape*) which appealed to the senses. Williams adopted 'sprung rhythm' from Hopkins, and yet he was not content to merely imitate his predecessor: '. . . let us do everything but be Influenced'.[96] *Taliessin Through Logres* and *The Region of the Summer Stars* offer ample evidence of the original style in which Williams applied the new technique, dividing whole-lines into small closed rhythmical units connected with one another by rhyme, alliteration, or assonance, by *cynghanedds*, or by other intricate figures of sound.[97]

Williams' tendency to use colloquial figures of speech is also traceable to Hopkins' influence.[98] The frequent use of ellipse and the extensive use of free word order tend to obscure easy comprehension of individual passages, and may even convey an initial impression of enigmatic crypticism. Only a close study of such passages can reveal the wealth of ideas and the musicality of language which lie behind the poetic art of Charles Williams: '. . . vainly Taliessin's first song / through river-mated rhythms while he smiled at the sky / pulsated; . . .'[99] Seen rhetorically, the above passage

96. *The Image of the City*, lxiii.

97. '. . . this, below them both, the shape of the blatant beast matched; . . .' ('Lamorack and the Queen Morgause of Orkney', in *Taliessin Through Logres*, 38-41, here 40).

    '. . . his voice / rove and drove words to the troth of ambiguous verse.' ('The Sister of Percivale', in *Taliessin Through Logres*, 51-3, here 51.

    '. . . to a plan / blown as that bone-patterned, bound each to a point. . . . its luck struck as her shoulders took the weight of the water.' ('The Sister of Percivale', 52).

98. Although Anne Ridler claims to have influenced the poet in this direction again and again.

99. 'The Calling of Taliessin', *The Region of the Summer Stars*, 5-20, here 5.

uses *hyperbaton*, that is to say a phrase alien to the original construction has been embedded in the matrix sentence, as a kind of parenthesis. But the figure is more than a mere mannerist device — it begins to echo of its own accord. The individual rhythmical units follow each other like the waves on a river, the accoustic form imitating the object represented. They cease ('song', 'rhythms') and begin anew ('through', 'while') and create the sense impression of pulsation, of recurrent natural movement. The reader is given the feeling that the song of Taliessin pulses like the waves of the river; it adjusts to the play of ripples on the water, gaining life and rising up from that same element, just as did Taliessin himself. Thus *hyperbaton* is revealed as a functional stylistic device used to underline the meaning of the poem.

Another characteristic of Williams' writing is his use of assonance, alliteration and internal rhyme. There are good reasons to doubt that such features could be explained without Hopkins, even though their use is totally Williams' own. This type of poetic diction does not appeal to everyone, many may even find it pretentious or artificial, and feel that the form distracts from the content:

> . . . my sister shall stand in his house
> to tend his daughter in the day of her destiny, but I
> make haste to Logres, to call and install King Arthur;[100]

Alliteration, internal rhyme, and assonance are all combined in this example. The use of internal rhyme corresponds to Williams' theoretical scheme of providing the non-strophic poems with two rhymes per line-pair, 'but these may be arranged as one wishes, . . .'[101] To my taste, Williams has overworked the device, above all in *Taliessin Through Logres*. Evidently the poet himself tired of such blatant pyrotechnics, for in 1941 he wrote:

> I do not find I altogether wish to continue using them,
> the verse of future poems may, I hope, be more sparing,
> . . . [102]

100. 'The Calling of Taliessin', 12.

101. *The Image of the City*, 183.

102. *The Image of the City*, 183.

The frequent use of compounded epithets is also reminiscent of Gerard Manley Hopkins, e.g. 'light-sprinkling', 'tiny-footed', 'bone-patterned'. There is a noticeable tendency towards parallelism and chiasm, paraphrase, leporism and oxymora, characteristics that point either directly to Hopkins, or, at the least, to a foible for 'Parnassian' language, as Hopkins liked to term his mannerisms. Anne Ridler is probably right in saying that 'Hopkins gave him a key to unlock resources which he already had'.[103] In any case, the new style introduced by Williams represented a valuable contribution to poetry. Hopkins gave Williams as an individual that which he had given the epoch as a whole: a healthy corrective against the over-moderation and self-complacency of Victorian poetic diction.

As significant as the use and development of such stylistic devices may be, it is Williams' unusual and unmistakable employment of metaphor that most reveals his personal signature. For Williams, metaphor was not merely one technique among others; it was the very soul of poetry, perhaps even its main determining characteristic. The poet would have concurred with every detail of what C. Day Lewis said on poetic imagery in the *Clark Lectures* (Cambridge, 1946):

> . . . every image re-creates not merely an object but an object in the context of an experience, and thus an object as part of a relationship. Relationship being in the very nature of metaphor, if we believe that the universe is a body wherein all men and all things are 'members one of another', we must allow metaphor to give a 'partial intuition of the whole world'. Every poetic image, I would affirm, by clearly revealing a tiny portion of this body, suggests its infinite extension.[104]

Lewis refers not only to the relationship between *tenor* and *vehicle*, that is the technique of poetic imagery, but also to the object of poetry, the world of the poet and seer (*vates*).

103. *The Image of the City*, 'Introduction', lxii.

104. C. Day Lewis, *The Poetic Image*. The Clark Lectures Given at Cambridge, 1946 (London, 1947), cited in Clifford Dyment, *C. Day Lewis*, Writers and their Work, No. 62 (London, 1969), 30.

170

The passage quoted calls up the figure of Taliessin to our mind's eye, and we see the organic body of the universe, the image which predominated in the thought and writing of Charles Williams. The image of the organic body provided him with a key to the nature of creation, and, at the same time, to the first and foremost task of poetry — to reveal the order of what appears to be chaos.

Thus the individual metaphor is to be interpreted as a cipher for a larger whole. It is meant to serve as a key to the illumination of truths beyond itself and beyond the natural, material world — to render them perceptible to the senses and comprehensible to the mind. Often these two steps follow so closely one upon the other that the actual metaphorical element gives way to the Platonic idea behind it; the pleasure in the musicality of the metaphor and its sensual appeal are transformed into a spiritual *analogia entis*.

In this characteristic focus on a transcendental *corpus* and on a supra-natural organic body lies the uniqueness of Williams' art of the metaphor. As a poet, he is neither a *homo faber* nor an *artifex* of daedalic art; instead, he is a seer and a prophet of hidden truths — a Platonic poet whose need of material for images which appeal to the senses exceeds the bounds of this earth.

The present-day reader will find Williams 'modern' where features of his style lead to esoteric ambiguity and to indirection in respect to the poetic meaning: the manneristic interlacing of convoluted thought patterns, the juxtaposition of disparate metaphors. But in contrast to other modern poets, the enigmatization of the message is oriented towards the topic, and upon closer study cryptic obscurity gives way to the sharp contours of objective clarity.

Nevertheless Williams is by no means a traditionalist, selecting earlier literary forms and materials for their usefulness, only to render them into the idiom of the contemporary. For this poet, the world of the Grail is not merely part of an ancient and venerable myth; it is an intellectual challenge, and a catalyst for concentration and reflection. Thus the Grail remains a symbol of the transcendental mystery, but the message Williams embues it with has nothing to do with the a-logical fascination of modern lyric poetry. Even those who do not respond to the message, who find it

171

old-fashioned,[105] unrealistic, and without appeal, cannot but admit that the poetic world created by Williams is coherent, comprehensible, and consistent.

It has often been noted that appreciation of the Arthurian works of Charles Williams depends on his world view and on his notion of man and his place in the universe. It is, of course, not very difficult to imagine where the negative critics of Williams are to be found. The anticipation of an atheistic, secular rejection of such a Christian work by sceptics sometimes leads to an apologetic, almost polemic stance on the part of sympathetic critics — one that Williams hardly requires.[106]

Indeed, the world of Williams is modern, vibrant with dynamic motion and spiritual anxiety. It is a portrait of mankind threatened by the forces and powers of destruction. In spite of the poet's adherence to Malory and his other medieval sources, the material has become a vehicle for a message of the twentieth century. This may well be due to the fact that Charles Williams has gained a deeper understanding of

105. The fact that Williams was accused of obscenity is a curiosity to be noted in passing. R. T. Davies voiced his reaction to reading Williams as follows: '. . . one would, if one had it at all, prefer one's pornography honest' ('Charles Williams and Romantic Experience', *Études Anglaises*, 8 (1955), 289-298, here 298). Such an accusation can hardly be taken seriously. At the same time, however, I would concede that the physiological symbolism in the *Arthuriad* does go a bit far. For instance, the idea that women offer a blood-sacrifice during menstruation and thus have a share in the sacrifice of Christ is, admittedly, ingenious, but hardly in good taste (cf. 'Prelude', *The Region of the Summer Stars*, 4). It appears to me that in this respect Williams belongs in the tradition of D. H. Lawrence and certain other English writers during the beginning of our century, who were resolved to combat the stigma of *prudery* through their explicit frankness.

106. For a particularly winning partisan defence of Williams, see Mary McDermott Shideler, *Charles Williams* (Grand Rapids, Mich., 1966). For a more detached view of Williams' relevance, see Barbara McMichael, 'Hell is Oneself: An Examination of the Concept of Damnation in Charles Williams' *Descent into Hell*', *Studies in the Literary Imagination*, 1 (Oct. 1968), 59-71. A particularly well-balanced and comprehensive account of Williams' philosophy and theology is to be found in Georgette Versinger's 'Charles Williams', *Études Anglaises*, 18 (July 1965), 285-295.

Arthurian mythology than any of his predecessors, and because he has given poetic voice to truths of which they were only subconsciously aware.

Williams, as a poet, has yet to come into his own. Some of the best minds of this century — among them fellow writers and friends, such as T. S. Eliot, Dorothy Sayers, Anne Ridler and John Heath-Stubbs — have recognized the profundity and the enormous scope of his vision. The scholar and friend who was closest to him in spirit — C. S. Lewis — has told us how to gauge the poetic achievement of *Taliessin Through Logres* and *Region of the Summer Stars*:

> They seem to me, both for the soaring and gorgeous novelty of their technique and for their profound wisdom, to be among the two or three most valuable books of verse produced in the century.[107]

107. C. S. Lewis, *Essays Presented to Charles Williams* (London, 1947), Preface, vi-vii.

William V. Spanos comes to the conclusion that Charles Williams deserves a better fate than to be dismissed as quaint or eccentric, see 'Charles Williams' *Seed of Adam*: The Existential Flight from Death', *Christian Scholar*, 49 (1966), 105-118.